A

SONG

FOR THE

RIVER

A

SONG

FOR THE

RIVER

PHILIP CONNORS

Cinco Puntos Press
El Paso, Texas

Grateful acknowledgment is made to the following for permission to reprint copyrighted material:

Patrice Mutchnick and the estate of Ella Jaz Kirk for excerpts from the writings of Ella Jaz Kirk, including "Cord Fluidity" and "A Prayer to the Raven," copyright © 2018 by Ella Jaz Kirk.

Counterpoint Press for an excerpt from the poem "The Lookouts," from *Left Out in the Rain* by Gary Snyder. Copyright © 1986 by Gary Snyder. Reprinted by permission of Counterpoint Press.

FIRST EDITION
10 9 8 7 6 5 4 3 2 1

Library of Congress Cataloging-in-Publication Data

Names: Connors, Philip, author.
Title: A song for the river / by Philip Connors.
Description: First edition. | El Paso, Texas : Cinco Puntos Press, [2018]
Identifiers: LCCN 2017057947| ISBN 9781941026908 (cloth : alk. paper) | ISBN 9781941026915 (paper : alk. paper) |
ISBN 9781941026922 (ebook) Subjects: LCSH: Connors, Philip. |
Fire lookouts—New Mexico—Gila National Forest—Biography. | Gila National Forest (N.M.) Classification: LCC SD421.25.C658 A3 2018 |
DDC 634.9/61809789692—dc23
LC record available at https://lccn.loc.gov/2017057947

Book and cover design by Anne M. Giangiulio
Cover photographs by Jay Hemphill

This is it! (Isn't that what you heard, Mary?)

Also by Philip Connors:

Fire Season: Field Notes From a Wilderness Lookout
All the Wrong Places: A Life Lost and Found

FOR MÓNICA

A Prayer to the Raven   15

A Hummingbird's Kiss   33

Birthday for the Next Forest   87

The Navel of the World   127

A Song for the River   179

Catechism for a Fire Lookout   217

IN MEMORIAM

JOHN KAVCHAR
Signal Peak Lookout · May 2012

ELLA SALA MYERS, MICHAEL SEBASTIAN MAHL, ELLA JAZ KIRK
Gila River · April 2014

Like any Romantic, I had always been vaguely certain that sometime during my life I should come into a magic place which in disclosing its secrets would give me wisdom and ecstasy—perhaps even death.
—Paul Bowles

The whole show has been on fire from the word go. I come down to the water to cool my eyes. But everywhere I look I see fire; that which isn't flint is tinder, and the whole world sparks and flames.
—Annie Dillard

A river loves the water / that it can never keep.
—Benjamin Alire Sáenz

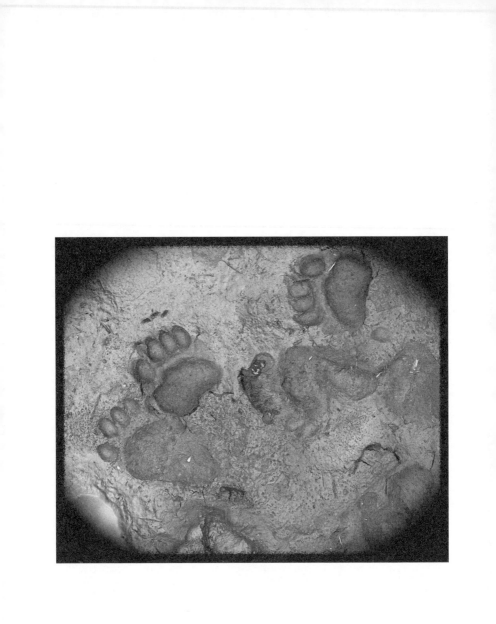

A PRAYER TO THE RAVEN

AFTER ILLNESS and divorce did a number on my body and soul, after wildfires burned the mountains and an airplane fell from the sky, after a horse collapsed on my friend and two hip surgeries laid me up for the better part of a year—loss piled on loss, pain layered over pain—I found I wanted nothing so much as to be near moving water.

So I went once more to the river.

The river emerges from springs and ice caves high in the mountains and gathers rain and snowmelt from a watershed of nearly 2,000 square miles. For more than a decade I had kept watch over those mountains and found the experience a two-hearted deal, living amid calamity and resilience. In the beginning I simply wished to remove myself from human company. I had my reasons, not at all unusual. But I kept returning for the communion of creatures that made my mountain hum, a beautiful Babylon of owls hooting and nutcrackers jeering and hermit thrushes singing their small and lovely whisper song—*a palace of organisms, a heaven for many beings, a temple where life deeply investigates the puzzle of itself,* as a wise man once said. The vultures, the ravens, the hawks, the Steller's Jays, the foxes

15

and bears, the elk and deer, the salamanders in their holes, the ladybugs in their tens of thousands: all of them were part of the mountain, and so were death and rebirth.

To watch a mountain you love murmur and chirp and howl and green up from rain and bloom with flowers, then see it succumb to flame and be blackened by heat only to live once more from the ashes, was to absorb an object lesson in transience and renewal. From my perch above the shaggy pines and stately firs, I looked down on a world burning itself up, most of us burning ourselves up in work and striving and the peculiar game of consumption and accumulation without end—the whole world on fire from our appetites and their cost—and I sometimes thought it would not be a terrible fate to lie down for the last time in ashes, preferably on a mountain.

On a mountain, ashes do not remain still for long. They are worked on by wind and water and follow ancient courses decreed by the laws of hydrology, which are determined by the laws of gravity. When enough of these watercourses converge in a form that pulses and recedes but does not cease, we call the convergence a river. In the mud along the banks of the river, mud dappled by the pawprints of bears, were remnants not just of the forests in the mountains but of people I had loved and admired, and their remnants also arrived there having been transfigured by flame to ash.

The river drew its shape from volcanic upheavals thirty-five million years ago, and for untold millennia creatures have gone about their mysterious business along its floodplain and in the substrate of its waters. Some of the mysteries have been revealed to us, thanks to people who make it their business to interpret them. I spent time with a team of biologists in the river that summer, wading hip deep in the big pools, watching their stream-dance as they high-stepped with dip nets and seine nets and hauled up fish to measure and count before returning them to the water unharmed.

They spoke of things they had learned—for instance how native loach minnows excavate a pocket beneath a flat rock in cobble. There the female lays her eggs for the male to fertilize. Being buoyant, the eggs adhere to the bottom of the rock. The male acts as the lookout over his progeny, cleaning away any fungus that attaches to the eggs and warding off insect predators and bottom-feeding desert suckers, until the eggs hatch and another generation takes its place in the weave of life that constitutes the river.

A threat hung over all this, another reason I went to the river. The threat appeared in the form of a concrete diversion dam that, if built, would put an end to the upper Gila River as a living entity. I wanted to find solace and strength in nearness to my friend John, a forest guardian while he lived, and my inspiration Ella Jaz, a river guardian while she lived, each of whom had gone before me in ash down the river—John after falling to his death beneath his horse, Ella Jaz after dying with her friends in the fiery wreckage of a plane. I wanted to hear, if I could, not just the voice of the river but the voices of my friend and inspiration, each of whom had known a thing or two about countering hubris and greed with logic and poetry. I wanted to pay homage to their memory as I rejoined the work of defending that sinuous green gallery of beauty from any attempt to defile it. I wanted to assure them we continued to speak up for the array of life that made the river sing—the yellow-billed cuckoo and the willow flycatcher and the spikedace minnow and the narrow-headed garter snake—in contrast to the bureaucrats, engineers, and county commissioners who uttered not an honest word in favor of the creatures that depended on the river, but instead sang hymns of praise to concrete berms, coanda screens, grouted boulder weirs, and prefabricated booster stations.

I wanted to see the river as it was and always had been, aware that men with power dreamed its death was nigh.

KNOWING I COULD stand a measure of frivolity amid my fear for the river and the obligations I felt to it and the dead, I called my friend the Swede and confirmed I was welcome for a visit to his lonely redoubt up a canyon in the headwaters. There I would be far enough upstream to have early warning were the river to rise and make feasible a float trip by boat. I took down a grocery list for the both of us and, provisioned for three weeks, set off on a drive ending beyond two locked gates and nine stream crossings.

"It's good to see you moving about," he said, as I hauled my coolers full of food onto the porch of the bunkhouse. "I thought you might have been lost forever down in the desert with your dubious hips and your shattered illusions."

Like others who are part of this story, the Swede was the sort who broke the mold. For as long as I had known him, he had spent his summers loafing about the Eagle Rock Ranch like some reprobate Buddha, babbling the days away, alternating between profundity and nonsense, although where one ended and the other began was not always clear. Occasionally he tired of his own voice and resumed a vow of silence: "I'm back in rehab," he would mutter, before retreating to a corner of the crumbling adobe bunkhouse with a cigar and a book, his last bladder bag of white wine abandoned to the recyling bin.

In a previous incarnation he had been a sort of anti-industrialist with a knack for dirty demolition work, and before that a lighthouse keeper in northern Sweden—the experience over which we first forged our connection, lighthouse keeper and fire lookout amounting to the same line of work if you swapped water for trees. Along with three partners he had built a small fortune using robots to dismantle nuclear reactors, steel plants, and other places where humans had found a way to heat, beat, and treat some industrial product. He had known both the sublime hush of the Baltic coast in deepest winter and the roar of heavy machinery in the act of high-dollar destruction; his company had repaired the ceiling of the Holland Tunnel between New Jersey and Manhattan and saved the Glen Canyon Dam spillway from the ruin of cavitation during the 1984 flood, an intervention for which I found it hard to forgive him. Without his robots working to hold it, the dam would have burst, re-exposing the drowned splendors of Glen Canyon.

"You should have let the thing crumble," I told him. "You would have been a hero. Ed Abbey would have kissed you."

"Emergency government money," he said. "It was a really tasty deal. But I do look back and wonder. My true calling was mycologist, but I ended up a garbologist. Someone had to clean up the disasters of industrial ingenuity."

After cashing out his share of the business in the mid-'90s, he sailed a boat around the world for nearly a decade, mostly in the south Pacific but also up and down the coast of Mexico. Rumor had it he had engaged in a little part-time smuggling to keep some skin in the game and not go flabby. As with most of the best characters I had met with some deep connection to the Gila River headwaters of southwest New Mexico, out on the ragged edge of the republic, he appeared to have lived his life in technicolor.

It was a verifiable fact, for instance, that he had served as the personal gofer, in San Francisco in the 1960s, to the manager of the Kingston Trio, a guy the Swede called by his first name only: Frank. Busted in possession of 258 pounds of marijuana during a police raid in 1968, Frank spent the rest of that strange decade in legal limbo. In the end he got off with a slap on the wrist.

A few years later Frank liquidated his various businesses—a record-production company, a restaurant, and several real-estate holdings, including San Francisco's Columbus Tower, which he sold to Francis Ford Coppola—and bought a plot of dreamland surrounded by the Gila Wilderness. There he spent the second half of his life chasing enlightenment and transcendence amid trickling hot spring seeps and pools alive with the movements of trout.

The Swede paid his first visit in 1976 and promptly fell in love with the place. He returned a couple of times a decade for the next forty years. He had abandoned the life of the oceans and returned to his native Sweden when the call came that Frank had died after a period of illness. The Swede got on a plane to the States, thinking he'd be gone a week or two in order to pay his respects to Frank's children.

Instead he stayed a decade.

The enchanting atmosphere of the canyon was the major thing that held him—that and the duty he felt to keep the place functioning now that Frank was buried on the mesa just above the stream. Since the ranch no longer had a permanent resident, the Swede feared it would fall into ruin if he didn't step in and tend to Frank's legacy. This fact may have accounted for our deepening bond, since I felt a similar devotion in regard to John and Ella Jaz, both also now joined in perpetuity with the river.

The Swede had perfected the life of the cot master, a vagabond creature capable of sleeping anywhere as long as he had a foldout cot, a sleeping pad, and a good mummy bag. The ranch offered him a stab at the ways of the bath master. Hot springs flowed from the ground all around, and some of them were tapped and redirected via hoses to a spot near the bank of the stream. The Swede took a profound and sustaining pleasure in maintaining a world-class private spa under semi-primitive conditions, running an array of siphons from horse trough to horse trough and ultimately to a clawfoot tub nestled in sedges and willows, keeping waters of various temperatures and pristine clarity available for soaking at all hours, in all weathers. He credited his continuing health in part to the therapeutic quality of those waters, and he tended to them like a lover.

Having judged me a kindred spirit on the basis of our shared experience of solitude, he let me know I was welcome at the ranch any time. I wasn't shy about making good on the offer. It was a place where you could always count on the welcome mental scouring of a good tequila drunk and ribald talk around an outdoor fire in the evenings, which together made for a nice anaesthetic for the sorrows of this world. Throw in some quality fishing, and those horse troughs arranged with a view down the canyon of burnt-sienna cliffs, and it was a trial run at Shangri-La. We had a standing agreement whereby he reimbursed me for the groceries,

I cooked all the meals, and he cleaned up afterward—the rest was play and minor maintenance. Now and then a water pipe would spring a leak and take four hands to fix by a method the Swede called "backcountry welding": inner-tube material, also known as "Mormon rawhide," cut in strips and wrapped around the leaky pipe with baling wire twisted over the top to hold the seal.

There were those who failed to understand my affection for the man, mutual acquaintances who viewed him as an unreconstructed ne'er-do-well, needlessly profane, a souse and a malingerer. It was true that he had neglected to sand off the rough edges of his persona, unlike most of us who bow to social pressure and an innate desire to please. But I have found it useful, for the sake of one's private morale, to have at least one friend who is not a better human than you are. Richer, sure. Older and wiser, fine. Just not better. We were both, he reminded me more than once, "lowlife white trash" of the northern European variety, and captive to our private dreams of freedom. But he was also something of a demented genius with the English language, a high priest in the secular practice of mirth.

Perhaps most crucially, he understood and honored the beauty of flowing water in an arid land.

Back in the canyon for the first time in more than a year, floating in the hot springs beneath the vastness of a sky unmarred by city lights, I made the Swede tell me all the old stories again—about Frank and San Francisco in the '60s, the lighthouse on the Baltic coast, his years in robot demolition—and I secretly dreamed of a wild run down the river.

I bided my time, waiting for the flood that would carry me and the ashes of the forest and the ashes of the dead on a journey that seemed like a prerequisite were I to feel fully alive again, after the loss of a marriage and a forest and a friend, all of them gone forever, and the loss of my mobility, thankfully only temporary. In the green light of dawn and the velvet dusk of evening, I took the healing waters in the tubs. By day I fished the glide runs and deep pools upstream and worked on improvements to a swimming hole, repositioning rocks, excavating sand and mud.

My own little diversion dam, I realized. My own little engineering project, playing with the flow, shaping it to my selfish purposes. A dream different from that of the schemers and boosters only in its scale and permanance.

My dam would burst with the next big rain in the headwaters. Theirs would mar the river forever.

IT WAS IN KEEPING with the history of the place that I should dream of a dam across the stream. A century earlier the property had been owned by a cattle baron of some renown, a British-born mining engineer and rancher who used it as his private retreat, forty miles upstream from his headquarters. Known to some by the sobriquet Thomas the Lion, the man controlled more than a million acres of rangeland at the height of his powers, attracting investors from London and New York, where he took a room at the Waldorf-Astoria when in town on business.

Back in his stronghold along the Gila River, he warred with rivals, evicted small landholders, and imposed his will, sometimes at gunpoint, on any who dared challenge him. When he discovered his first wife sharing intimacies with another man, he promptly shot the man dead, without consequence from local law, which deferred to him in most matters of life and property.

As sometimes happens to such men, Thomas the Lion died from

a hammer blow to the skull, his body dumped in a ravine off a side street in El Paso, Texas, in 1917, after which his empire crumbled.

While he still had the ability to dream his dreams of dominance, he had imagined a dam on the river's main stem. With partners he went so far as to incorporate the Gila River Power Company in February 1910, with the goal *to generate, sell, distribute and transmit power for mining, milling, manufacturing, lighting, heating and other purposes, either by steam, electricity, water power, or any other means whatsoever.* That was in keeping with his methods: by any means whatsoever. The dam would have stood 200 feet tall, with a span across the canyon of 1,000 feet. It would have funneled the river through a nine-foot-diameter pipe across a length of nearly seven miles from the point of diversion to an off-site reservoir with a capacity of more than 217,000 acre feet—or enough water to fill, to a depth of twelve inches, the surface area of 217,000 football fields. Like other such ideas that came after, it foundered on the shoals of cost and logistics.

I thought of the cattle baron as I wrestled with rocks on what was once his private getaway, deepening my swimming hole, forming the perfect curvature on the wall of my dam. God knows what crazy scheme the scoundrel might have come up with had he lived another twenty years, what fresh disaster of industrial ingenuity, but the sad fact was a new generation had revived the old dream of a dam on the Gila, and this time they had a big pile of money and real political power—not to mention a thirst for water that had about it a whiff of dipsomania.

WE SHALL RETURN, in due time, to their methods and their madness, but for now we must leave them to one side of the story, just as I was happy to leave behind all thought of them on the day the rain began in earnest in the canyon that September, the cleansing power of a flood clearly imminent. The dying remnants of Hurricane Newton moved up from the Gulf of California to saturate the mountains, rain falling for twenty-four hours straight. I knew my time had come—time to honor John and Ella Jaz with a fool's journey down the river alone, kept company only by my memory of their words and the presence in the water of their ashes. The headwaters began to swell with runoff. I watched my dam start to buckle. I said adios to the Swede and told him I'd be back by the end of the week if my inflatable Sea Eagle proved up to the rigors of one more Wilderness run.

It took me a day to prepare. I had staged my boat at the Swede's *pied-à-terre* back in town on my way to see him up the river, thinking of precisely this moment, so I hauled it out of his basement and gathered the necessary food and supplies, dry bags and lifejacket, camp stove and sleeping bag. With the help of a friend, I parked my truck at the take-out spot on the far side of the Wilderness so I would have wheels at the end of the journey. Then I drove back toward the headwaters in a truck I had borrowed from the Swede. In the shadow of the bridge where the forks of the river converged, I inflated the boat with a bellows pump and packed and strapped down my dry bags. All the while the river kept rising, its waters the color of coffee with a splash of cream. Burnt logs from the burn scars in the mountains bobbed past and joined for a while with a miniature jam at the base of the bridge, only to burst free when a big one plowed into the mess of limbs and trunks and other flotsam, and the force dislodged the whole thing and sent it scattering and scalloping in the current.

The sun had re-emerged, the sky dotted with a few brilliant white clouds. The river sang its sibilant song of high water.

I skidded the boat across the sand to the water's edge and jumped aboard, off and running in the flow.

THE GILA is one of the undersung glories of boating in the American West. In its upper reaches it is a true Wilderness run: no hand-holding river rangers, no telling in advance where the hazards lurk. Its rapids, nearly alone among such rivers, remain unnamed. There exists no guidebook devoted to itemizing its dangers or highlighting the hot springs and camp spots along its banks. Local intelligence can be had if you know the right people, but mostly you are on your own, and anyway the river's mood can change in a moment. It is only floatable at flood stage, meaning you can rarely plan a trip ahead of time, and at flood stage it can be unpredictable hour to hour.

A group of river rats I knew, a family of innkeepers from Gila Hot Springs and one of their neighbors, had jumped on it three years earlier at what they thought was high water after an autumn thunderstorm, unaware a major logjam had formed upstream in one of the headwater forks. Heavy rain had flushed tons of burned snags into the watershed, and the jam held back enormous quantities of water. When it burst it caused the river to jump from less than 5,000 cubic feet per second (cfs), still a significant flood of the sort seen only every few years, to almost 30,000 cfs, the fourth-highest flow ever recorded on the upper Gila River in ninety years of measurements.

The river rats pulled their crafts off the stream and sought high ground as dead trees and debris roared by like a locomotive of hydrologic energy.

"We were not going to play bumper cars with that," one of them later told me. After the debris flow passed, they jumped in their boats and rode the back side of the wave, almost certainly the wildest journey ever undertaken by humans on that stream.

A few days later, some friends of mine set off on a nine-day run from the confluence of the river's forks all the way to Safford, Arizona, a trip whose second half would no longer be possible if the dam were built.

My ride occurred at a flow of around 1,200 cfs, which was plenty hairy enough for my skill set—I had only been down the Wilderness portion of the river one other time. The first few hours were glorious, just me and the river and the knowledge that with me in the river were the remnants of John and Ella Jaz, all of us carried along together by a force older by far than anything human: rain running downhill and converging in the form of a river. Water moved all around, pouring in rivulets over the lip of the canyon, and the willow brush in the floodplain bent and shivered with the force of it where the river jumped the channel and braided across the bottomlands. I dodged a strainer and skirted several sweepers hanging low over the surface, alders and cottonwoods reaching down with their branches to touch the stream like crooked fingers. I tried to stay in tune with the moment and the wishes of the river, tried to stay centered in the main channel.

When I saw a raven circling and soaring over the canyon ahead of me, I thought of some words I had once read by Ella Jaz—

I prayed to the Raven.
I asked him to help me get wings to fly.
To help me be rebellious like him.
To help me see the world from above but be part of it too.

Before she left us she had indeed taken flight like the raven, soaring over the forest on a mission of watchfulness. She had rebelled with dignity in protest against those who schemed of damming the Gila. She had seen the world from above and joined, too soon, with her very favorite part of it, by going in ash with the river.

Before long, thoughts of prayer would come to me too.

IT WAS AN ALDER that knocked me akilter, or rather a pair of alders, each a simple sweeper hanging low above the current. I saw the first coming too late, so I ducked and hoped. I sat up just in time to see the second and duck again. Its branches brushed against the boat and turned it sideways. Before I could right the ship, it ran up against a log held in place by a hillock of grass on what had three days before been dry floodplain, but in those three days the flow had increased more than twenty-fold. The boat snuggled up against the log and paused there, perpendicular to the current, suspended ever so briefly while all around it water moved—and then it filled and flipped.

I went under for a moment, popped to the surface like a cork, went under again and came up coughing and spitting, searching for something to grab hold of, but there was nothing but moving water and me moving with it. The boat floated upside down behind me. I could see a water jug bobbing and the bellows pump sinking, and I no longer held my paddle in my hands. For a hundred yards I swept along helplessly until I managed to grab onto the boat and push it into a slackwater eddy in a sharp bend of the river, where I hauled myself and my craft onto shore.

I shivered from some combination of cold and fear, awed by

the force of the river, grateful it hadn't swallowed me whole or spit me out mangled.

On a flat bench above the high water mark, I stripped off my clothes and hung them on limbs of oak and juniper. I built a fire, unstrapped and unpacked my dry bags, and took stock of the shape I was in. Half my drinking water: gone with the river. No big deal, since I knew the location of good springs downstream. My bellows pump: gone in the river. No big deal as long as my sorry little rubber ducky didn't puncture over the next thirty miles.

My paddle: gone down the river…

I took a moment to wonder at what a fool I was, not having brought a spare. It was a rookie move, a pretty serious piece of carelessness or arrogance or both—as if my benevolent posture toward the river were enough to protect me from its dangers, as if it would understand I meant it no harm and would do me no harm in return.

Up the river without a paddle!

With a mixture of curiosity and dread, I marked the river's edge with a stick. I spread some loose tobacco from a waterlogged pouch on a rock next to my fire. When it dried I rolled a smoke and cracked a beer and boiled some water for dinner—a freeze-dried backpacker's meal, followed by a Clif bar for dessert.

I sat with my back against a log and watched the river as darkness drew down on the canyon.

In an hour the marker stick was gone, carried away on the gathering flood.

I DID NOT PRAY, although I was tempted for the first time in decades. I did not panic, although I felt the press of fear against my throat like the dull edge of a knife.

I was twenty-seven river miles upstream from a road, ten miles downstream from one, and there would be no turning back. I had committed—and I needed a paddle.

That night around my fire, I spoke to John and Ella Jaz, whose remnants in the river gave me a peculiar form of comfort: if my time to join the river was now, we would have ourselves a reunion in eternity. It wasn't a macabre idea—just a fact—but after entertaining the notion for a little while, I came around to a conviction of sorts, the best I could muster under the circumstances. In the morning, I told myself and them, I would fashion a makeshift oar from driftwood and bark held together by Gorilla Tape, the last thing I grabbed when I left the Swede's place in town, almost an afterthought at the time, now quite possibly a lifesaver. In order to preserve the integrity of my cowboy oar, I would only steer with it, never paddle, simply going with the flow, surrendering to the wishes of the river until I too was of a piece with the river—either on it or in it.

If I was lucky enough to make it out the other side using gifts of the river's gallery forest to navigate its flow, I vowed to finish the story of the fires in the mountains and the ashes in the watershed, braiding it together with stories of the river and the dead—their beauty and their grace, their passion and their purpose—and I would make an offering of the story in the hope it would touch others as they had touched me.

The next day's journey was so enchanting that to fix it in words would only diminish it. Perhaps it will suffice to say that I made it unharmed—and along the way the river answered questions I had never thought to ask. Will a deer swim when startled by a man in a boat? Might grace arise from fear? Can water talk to water?

This, then, is the story I owed the river and the dead.

A HUMMINGBIRD'S KISS

I THOUGHT I HEARD a shout from somewhere far below me. Snug in the cocoon of my sleeping bag, face averted from the honey-colored sunrise pouring through the windows, I could not at first remember where I was and why. For a moment I experienced the tingly, dissociative terror one feels upon waking from a bad dream—only to realize I was waking into one.

The shout came twice more before I linked the voice with one of the few people I could imagine greeting with open arms under the circumstances. It belonged to Teresa, fiancée of my friend John, whom we had been missing, cursing, and mourning for three weeks. She had started up the mountain before daybreak, a steep, two-and-a-half-mile hike from the trailhead on the highway. Sleep eluded her past about three in the morning anymore, so she found ways to make use of the dawn hours, fueled by plenty of coffee. For me the trouble was the night, but I sedated myself in the customary manner.

Although her days of paid fire watch were behind her, Teresa still surpassed me by almost two decades of lookout experience, having worked thirty seasons in total, most of them in the Gila, our shared home forest. She last occupied a tower in the Gila the year before I wandered into the country. My rookie season coincided with her venturing north to work lookouts in Oregon and Idaho, so I had missed out on the pleasure of hearing her voice over my two-way radio. Hearing it now, in person, I felt sorrow and gratitude at once. The sorrow would have been there with or without her presence, but I was grateful I needn't hide it from her, as I would have from the average day hiker. On the contrary I could share it with her, and share in hers. Perhaps we could dull the edge of it for each other just a little.

During a dozen summers on lookout, I had mostly spent my nights in a cabin in another mountain range twenty miles away, but there was no cabin on John's peak, only the tower—a spacious live-in model. I invited Teresa up the stairs, feeling funny at having to proffer the invitation. She had spent far more time here, hanging out with John, than I ever had; I was merely an emergency fill-in, on loan from the neighboring ranger district. A fire there the previous summer had burned a couple hundred square miles all around my lookout tower, which now had the feel of a bird's nest marooned in a charscape. Not a lot remained that could still catch fire in that country, so my boss figured he could spare me for a few weeks while I covered John's shifts, and my relief lookout worked extra to cover mine.

I slipped into my pants and went hunting for my hat while Teresa's hiking boots rang on the tower's metal steps. Given her intimate understanding of the profession, she refused to climb an occupied lookout without permission from its resident caretaker, aware that fire towers in our part of the world serve not merely as scenic overlooks for tourists, but as actual work spaces for lookouts, some of whom consider pants a sartorial extravagance.

Rare is the pleasure hiker whose love of the wild in all its manifold splendor is capacious enough to include a surprise confrontation with a hairy human ass. Nonetheless, I had discovered that an unsettling number of visitors to John's mountain disregarded the sign at the base of the tower, which informed the curious that the structure had an official purpose, and that permission was required to climb it during its annual period of occupancy, roughly April through August. People being people, some ignored the official verbiage and began their thoughtless trudge up the steps without even a shout of hello. Maybe this impertinence could be pinned on the implausibility, in our day and age, of some lucky bastard still getting paid by the US government to stare out the window at mountains all day; maybe some people could no longer be troubled to read from a surface other than a screen. In any event, when John had ruled the roost he would intercept trespassers partway in their ascent and inform them that he was just about finished with some very important and time-sensitive government paperwork. He would be glad to share the view if only they would wait at the base of the tower for ten or fifteen minutes—twenty tops—while he dotted the *I*s and crossed the *T*s. After this harmless but satisfying exercise in territorial pissing, he would abruptly return to his glass-walled perch on stilts and laugh to himself. The fact that our job demanded no such thing was part of what we loved about it.

I joined Teresa on the catwalk, where she stood very still next to the hummingbird feeder, loose-limbed but confident in her posture, her cheeks burnished pink from the exertion of the hike. Once the bird she was studying zoomed away, she fixed her pale blue eyes on the horizon, searching in the habitual way of lookouts for a wisp of smoke, a low-flying plane. Her ginger-colored hair and freckled face made her look a decade younger than she was. Our brief acquaintance had revealed that her tolerance for macho bluster was the inverse of her capacity for solitude, and her capacity for solitude was as large as any I knew. I had seen her verbally fillet more than one fool who had highlighted his foolishness with a bigoted phrase or a fraudulent argument after one too many cocktails—a wit that could slice with a scalpel's precision being a useful implement for a woman who tended to move in realms pungent with testosterone. She laughed at her own jokes with unrestrained delight and feared nothing that I could discern. More than once since we met, I had found myself thinking that I wanted to be like her when I grew up.

We leaned against the catwalk railing, facing north toward the Gila River and the mountains that gave birth to it. Tinsel tufts of ground fog traced the creases in the land, the major canyons and the creek valleys. It was one of those mornings of fresh-scrubbed serenity that made the forest look like a world at the dawn of time—a view, from where we stood, so magnanimous with earthly beauty it made me want to live forever, even as I was more aware than usual of the fact that I would not.

In the middle distance we could see the southern half of the Gila Wilderness, the original American experiment in shielding wild country from the appetites of the machine age. In 1924, as an idealistic young forester, Aldo Leopold convinced his superiors in the Forest Service to create a buffer around the only mountains left in the American Southwest not carved up by roads and keep them that way. His plan made the land surrounding the Gila River headwaters the world's first Wilderness with a capital W, off limits to automobiles and tourist developments, a place where all travel demanded the exertions of animate flesh, either one's own or that of a horse. This exercise in willed restraint had preserved, for ninety years and running, a big enough stretch of country to allow for a pack trip with mules lasting two weeks, during which the pack string never had to cross a road or its own tracks.

Even if Leopold weren't venerated as a sort of high priest in the new religion of ecology, having changed the way we think about the natural world thanks to his visionary land ethic, he would be remembered for changing the terms of our relationship with some pretty big chunks of it—none more resonant with symbolism than the Gila. For some of us it was not only the first Wilderness but one of the best: a beautifully jumbled land of mountains, mesas, and deeply incised canyons, the major wildland bridge connecting the southern Rockies with the northern Sierra Madre, and a place of rich biological mixing where life from the Nearctic realm mingled with migrants from the Neotropical.

Teresa had explored as much of that Wilderness as anyone I knew. I never tired of hearing her stories of riding the trails with grizzled mule packers or running the river's forks solo in a battered boat. These were uncommon pursuits, to put it mildly. Packing with mules had always been a specialized skill, and those who boated on the river did so on the Gila's main stem, not its smaller headwater tributaries. The forks were considered too small, offered too many challenges, involved too much boat-dragging and bushwhacking of the sort that could elicit four-letter words from a river-running nun. I hadn't heard of anyone else even attempting such a float in recent years.

For Teresa, the allure of a run down the forks resided in the difficulty, partly, and the novelty, partly, but also in the guarantee of solitude in a place unsullied by the filth and flotsam of *Homo economicus*. It was harder all the time to get away from the casual sadism that inflected so much of American life, but a boat trip down one of the forks of the Gila was one sure way to do it. Hers was that rare sensibility as undomesticated as the landscape. In most of her major life decisions, she had been guided by an innate attraction to wild creatures and untamed country, making for a life lived around ranchers and firefighters and others who worked outdoors—fuel-wood cutters and horse breeders and such of their ilk. A self-described "feral child with few social graces" in her youth in suburban Arizona, she had become what was called an old Gila hand: *hand* being the most respectful moniker bestowed on humans in wild country, and *old* not an epithet but an honorific.

As the Swede once put it admiringly, having fallen a little bit in love, "She was born without a bourgeois bone in her body."

Her forays out from under rooftops had not been limited to the Gila. I came to think of her life as a long, peripatetic journey through what was left of wild America, and aside from mountain lookouts, rivers were the thread that ran through it. She had once floated the Green River solo, from northern Utah to Lake Powell, 430 miles in six weeks—one of many such trips on streams all over the country, including the Pelican in northern Minnesota and the Big Bend of the Rio Grande down in Texas. She had also ridden horseback across the southern island of New Zealand and done the same from Mexico to Canada, a six-month journey on the second day of which she was dragged by a rope that connected her horse to a temperamental mule barely green-broke. Amid the commotion she suffered a fractured arm. For most people that mishap would have derailed the trip, or at least postponed it, but Teresa was not most people. As fortune would have it, she found her way to a nearby ranch owned by a semi-professional rodeo cowboy who kept a supply of casting material handy in his tack shed. He used it on the calves he practiced roping when the rope broke one of their legs. Calf-roping tended to result in a fair number of broken legs, which healed relatively quickly when properly set. His expertise made for an impeccable cast on her arm; he sent her on her way with some extra plaster, in case the cast wore out and she needed to make a replacement herself. Four weeks later she did just that.

But that was long ago, in what sometimes seemed to her another life entirely. During one of her last seasons as a lookout, she came unglued after too much time spent in a poisoned tower. The previous occupant had died when he fell off a sheer cliff below the lookout for reasons unknown. The mystery of his death became a little less mysterious after Teresa began suffering from memory loss, asthma attacks, and extreme bouts of vertigo. A mycologist who was called in on a hunch from the University of Oregon identified the culprit: toxic black mold growing behind the tower's wall panels. As if that weren't an exotic enough malady, a tick bite later bequeathed her a bouquet of blood-borne pathogens. This, combined with the mold poisoning, set her on a self-directed medical odyssey that lasted several years and only really delivered relief after she made a practice of lying very still in a hyperbaric chamber. In the worst of her anguish, she had stood on a bridge over the Colorado River on a lonely summer night and imagined herself for one final moment a bird, swooping toward the canyon bottom in what she later wryly noted would have been terminal velocity. It was, in its weird way, a happy thought—flying like that, launching into the afterlife. It cheered her so much she decided it had to be one of those beautiful human ideas, of which we have so many, that are better in theory than in practice.

At age sixty-three, having lived hand-to-mouth for decades in order to feed her jones for adventure and avoid what she viewed as the suffocating expectations of the culture, namely marriage and motherhood, she surprised herself by having a change of heart about marriage. (John surprised himself too, having recently left a seven-year relationship that didn't result in an exchange of vows.) With her capacity for solitude and all-around hardihood, she made a felicitous match with John—her groundedness a nice balance for his occasional flights of fancy—but they had been granted only eleven months together, just long enough to know they wanted it to last. In a matter of weeks she had gone from the novelty of imagining forever with one man to confronting forever without him: from wedding engagement to memorial service. She had hosted, with grace and good humor, grieving family members from out of state and guided John's body from autopsy to cremation. Now she was walking around with his ashes in a gallon freezer bag and looking, uncharacteristically, a little bit lost.

It had the feel of an appropriate day for spreading some of those ashes. The breeze was no more than a whisper in the tops of the pines below us. Their needle clusters glinted like tiny pom poms as they caught the slanted sunlight. With the ribbons of ground fog beginning to dissolve, we turned our attention southward, where we could see mountains over in southeast Arizona and down along the Mexican border—Gadsden Purchase land, the final chunk of territory added to the Lower 48. It was a lonely and sun-seared

40

country and in some ways the last American frontier, a place where ranchers, smugglers, and migrants tested their resolve against a pitiless landscape long on rock and short on water.

We both felt the gravity of what we were about to do and so held off a while longer, not wanting to rush toward a reckoning. Instead we remained on the catwalk and watched the forest come alive with the songs of morning, sometimes speaking quietly to each other, sometimes pointing to something in the landscape, sometimes standing silently attentive as the hummingbirds buzzed around the feeder and the shadows shortened and the air began to warm.

I left Teresa alone with the view and went inside the tower to make myself some oatmeal and a cup of coffee, extra strong, with a generous pour of cream to mask the bitterness. As I warmed my hands on the cup and felt my blood quicken with caffeine, the other lookouts began to call in service over the radio—first Jean's voice, then Hedge's, and on around the horn, one by one, nine of them in all, until each of us had been accounted for but me. Some days I liked to speak first and others I preferred to go last, and often the ritual round of morning voices called to mind the first few lines of Gary Snyder's poem "The Lookouts":

Perched on their bare and windy peaks
They twitter like birds across the fractured hills
Equipped by science with the keenest tool—
A complex two-way radio, full of tubes.

The most alone, and highest in the land,
We trust their scrupulous vision to a man:

Likely in Snyder's time and place, the lookouts had all been men, but on the Gila in the 21st century the gender split was roughly fifty-fifty, and the lookouts I admired most were women. Four of them—Teresa, Jean, Sara, and Rázik—counted a hundred fire seasons worth of experience altogether, a deep reservoir of knowledge about the work and the country that, one had to believe, would never again be duplicated.

Jean had once lived alone on a boat off the Virgin Islands and taught in Detroit city schools. Unmoored after a breakup with a man she assumed she would marry, she came to feel her only hope for salvation resided in the freedom of the open road and the stark beauty of the American desert. She drifted southward across the country in her Isuzu pickup, sleeping in the back under a camper shell, until she came to rest in Truth or Consequences, New Mexico, where she decided to put down roots. The name of the place appealed to her, as did the clarity of the sky and the naked geology of the mountains. Now in her forties, she had spent one-third of her summers on Earth working the loneliest of the Gila's lookout peaks. She saw fewer visitors than the rest of us by far, sometimes only three or four during a whole fire season.

Sara and Ráz split time equally on their mountain. The hike in was so long—twelve miles—it didn't make sense for one of them to work the relief lookout's schedule of four days every two weeks, only to spend two full days coming and going on the trail. Sara had first come into the country during a 3,000-mile thru-hike along the Continental Divide from Mexico to Canada, back in 1980, before there was a properly marked CDT. She had worked more summers on her mountain, thirty-three straight, than John and I combined on ours. She figured she could hang up her binoculars without regret once she reached the nice round number of fifty fire seasons. Ráz liked to say that Sara knew the lay of the land so well she could tell you precisely which tree had caught the lightning that started the fire.

At twenty-four seasons of service herself, Ráz was no slouch when it came to understanding the country. She had a previous career in government shipyards, the only woman on crews installing communication systems in submarines. Now she was in her seventies and spry as most people half her age—a little slower on the hike to reach the tower than she was once upon a time, but still hardcore. And I do mean hardcore. In one recent fire season, she had walked to and from her lookout half the summer on a broken foot.

I joined the morning chorus by pressing the transmit button on my Bendix-King VHF radio full of tubes and carefully enunciating, "Silver City Dispatch, Signal Peak, in service." It felt peculiar, almost a form of sacrilege, to mimic those seven little words John had uttered on more than a thousand mornings, but Signal Peak was where I was, so that's who I was, for the time being.

ONCE I FINISHED calling in the weather, Teresa suggested a morning stroll. We descended the tower and walked down the trail until we came to an opening in the forest, where the ridge overlooked the rounded peaks of the Twin Sisters to the south. John had come there often with his wife, back when they first staffed the lookout, back when Miquette was still alive. In 1999 she had been hired as the primary lookout, he as her relief, and they both came to cherish the view from a natural stone bench just below the top of the ridge: ponderosa pine rolling down the slopes of the Pinos Altos Range, giving way eventually to piñon and juniper, and beyond them the cougar-colored grasslands. Miquette's tenure lasted just four summers. In 2003, half a year after her death, John spread some of her ashes in the clearing.

Now it was his time to join her.

In their last months together, John played caretaker while Miquette succumbed to cancer. I didn't know him at the time, except as one of the many voices on my two-way radio. He later told me it was the most difficult thing he had ever done—and the most meaningful. Tending to the needs of a dying lover surpassed any form of intimacy he had known, even as it tested the limits of his emotional and physical strength. According to people in a position to know, he did with patience and tenderness a thing he hated having to do at all, which is perhaps one way of defining the outer reaches of unconditional love: grace in the face of the unbearable.

A surprise bequest from Miquette's godmother had granted the two of them the freedom to live on the road for years, untethered to the demands of gainful employment. They had dropped anchor in different campgrounds full of vagabonds for a week or a month at a time, moving across the mountains and deserts of the West, from Arizona to Idaho, Colorado to California, a habit they kept up in the offseason after they became lookouts. It felt crucial that their final journey not end in some godforsaken institutional room. Once they learned the cancer was incurable, they made a plan for what John called "hospice in a motor home." Ignoring her doctor's appalled warnings to the contrary, they packed up her crutches and oxygen tanks, her gauze patches and pill bottles, and set off toward a secret camp they both loved in Death Valley.

It was as romantic, in its own intimate way, as a honeymoon, John later wrote of that week, in an essay he published in a newsletter for RV enthusiasts, likely the most moving piece of writing ever to appear in its pages.

They continued west to a campground on the Pacific coast, where the host, apprised of their situation, waived the two-week stay limit. As was their way, they kept making new friends until the very end. Fellow campers came by to see if they needed help; some brought tapioca pudding to share with Miquette, aware she couldn't eat much else. When the end drew near, they bowed to necessity and joined her family in Santa Cruz. *On New Year's Eve, with a sigh, Miquette slipped gently away,* John wrote. *Outside the bedroom window, fireworks sparkled in the midnight sky.*

Afterward John felt an urge to bend his grief to some redeeming purpose, so he signed on as an air angel, flying sick patients in need of emergency medical care to distant hospitals free of charge in his own private plane. He reminded himself that although the end had come too soon for her—she had gone at the age of fifty-six—Miquette had managed to live out her dreams. As a little girl she fantasized about living one day in a treehouse and loved horses so much she wanted to be one. After she met John, they lived in the shadow of 14,000-foot peaks in Colorado, tucked amid a grove of aspens on the edge of an alpine meadow, where they worked as caretakers of a large horse herd. Later they took up seasonal residence on Signal Peak, in a sort of deluxe treehouse above the Gila. The timing and manner of her death had not undone the fact that hers had been, in so many ways, a charmed life.

So had John's, mostly. As with all of us, there were corners of his personal history shadowed in varying degrees of darkness, but on the day of his death, age sixty-two, he was happier than he had been in some time, excited to be planning a honeymoon that would involve flying his Cessna Cardinal around the American West with Teresa so they could golf in a different state each day on a lark—a major concession on her part, golf being far afield of her own interests.

But what the hell, the things we do for love.

Instead the plane sat orphaned in a hangar at the Grant County Airport, and there would be no teeing off in Arizona one day and Utah the next, not to mention no more air angel flights with him at the controls.

SITTING ON THE STONE BENCH, Teresa and I sifted through what we remembered most vividly about John. His laughter still echoed in our memories, and often we felt like displaced conduits for it. Never one to be stingy with his emotions, he would have approved of us crying one minute and giggling the next—and sometimes both at once.

I often thought of him as the blue-eyed gringo incarnation of a Mudhead Kachina, the drumming, dancing clown in Hopi ceremonies: partial to mischief and merriment, and the most gregarious lover of solitude I had ever known. His laughter, his most winning characteristic, tumbled forth in staccato waves, his belly shaking, his torso rocking back and forth from the hinge of his waist like a see-saw. It was a sort of bebop laugh that reminded me of a Dizzy Gillespie solo—supple and exuberant, the individual notes crowding each other as if in a hurry to be free in the world. When children visited his lookout tower, he delighted in showing them how he could make a flower of his lips by painting them with lipstick and pursing them just so, luring hummingbirds for a kiss if he stood as still as a statue on the catwalk. I found the tube of cherry-colored Wet *n* Wild in the drawer where he stored his weather instruments. Its gauche branding at first made me laugh and then ruined me for half an hour with all it evoked of him.

The sight of that lipstick was nothing compared with my initial glimpse of his handwriting in the logbook, which detailed the major events of his last hours alive:

> *Noonish—Past lookout Bart Mortenson family arrives. Bart was a lookout here in the 70s. He honeymooned here*
> *12:32—Smoke report: Azimuth 247° 30', Township 16S, Range 14W, Section 32—small white column—call it BART FIRE*
> *12:39—Smoke more dense, still white color*
> *12:57—Engine 672 on scene*
> *13:00—Mortenson family spreads Bart's ashes north of tower. Nice singing of hymns drifting inside…*
> *19:00—Out of service*

In addition to ruing everything unsaid and undone, the mind can't help but hunt for crumbs of solace in the aftermath of an unforeseen death. I found mine in the fact that, like Miquette, John had eluded the confines of a grim hospital chamber for his end. Shortly after writing the words *Out of service*, he saddled his horse Sundance and set off on a ride along the Continental Divide, passing by the spot where he had spread Miquette's ashes eleven years earlier. He had promised to ring Teresa that evening but never did. She tried him multiple times, but the call always went straight to voice mail. When he didn't report in service over the radio the next morning, Teresa met up with two of his closest friends—his relief lookout, Mark Johnson, and his supervisor, Keith Matthes. They set out ahead of a search-and-rescue team in a hunt for him, while Teresa went straight to the lookout tower.

The hunt did not last long. Keith discovered John and the horse in the position they had fallen, less than a mile from the tower. Sundance had collapsed to the downhill side of the trail and crushed John beneath him. Neither showed signs of having struggled. Death for both appeared instantaneous. Those of us who loved John told ourselves that whatever the reason for the fall—the evidence, according to Keith and Mark, suggested a horse heart attack, although we would never know for sure—he had gone quickly, while doing something he enjoyed, in a place he loved.

June 7, 2014, just happened to be the day he did so.

"At least he died with his boots on," I glibly told Teresa, when we met in the hours after his body was found.

"Not quite," she said. "Classic John: the bastard was wearing his tennis shoes. If he'd had his boots on, who knows, he might've got out of the stirrups in time."

When she later visited the scene, she found cause to develop her own theory about the fall. It involved Sundance's habit of rearing on his hind legs, a habit she had warned John was dangerous and ought to be nipped in the bud. She noticed two freshly sawed logs next to the trail a little ways ahead of the place where Sundance collapsed. The logs had been dropped by firefighters less than a month earlier, and the entire hillside was still black from the fire they had battled. She figured Sundance came around the bend and saw the ends of those cut logs looking like big googly eyeballs or two white moons. "I'm guessing he got spooked and reared," she said. "And because of the fire, the footing there wasn't great. Keith told me he noticed that Sundance's neck was bent between two saplings. I think he fell awkwardly and broke it, and that was that."

THOSE OF US with long experience sitting watch over the Gila sometimes joked that we weren't so much fire lookouts anymore as we were pyromaniacal monks or morbid priests—officiants at an ongoing funeral for the forest we had found when we first assumed our posts. All of us had been attracted to the job for its promises of solitude and adventure, the romance of wild mountains and a taste of the sublime. It delivered everything we hoped for and more, including a privileged view of wildfire on a landscape scale. The season never lasted long enough—six months maximum, more like three or four in a typical year—but it beat hustling for a living down in the neon plastic valleys.

Nationwide our numbers dwindled by the year, our sort of work a casualty of "development" and the never-ending schemes of the techno-titillated, who looked forward to the day when the last of us would be put out to pasture by satellites, drones, and high-definition infrared cameras linked with pattern-recognition software. Sometimes it seemed an oversight on the part of the culture that the job still existed at all.

Even in the eyes of some of our friends, we lookouts were considered a little bit goofy—but we were blessedly so, having found a job where being a little bit goofy was a prerequisite. In the sunset days of a doomed vocation, we had lucked into a lineage of mountain mystics and lone rangers. We were paid in US dollars to read the meaning in clouds and discern the difference between a smoke and a water dog, and those of us who kept with it across the decades became walking repositories of bird-migration and weather patterns, fire history and trail conditions. We performed annual maintenance on our facilities and for days and sometimes weeks on end luxuriated in silence and solitude. Some of us even learned to kiss hummingbirds.

Then a thunderstorm moved over and the fires busted out, two or three or a dozen in an afternoon, and we earned our keep triangulating the coordinates of smokes, alerting crews to sudden changes in wind and fire behavior, and guiding smokejumpers toward good trails on which to hike out after demob. It was hard to imagine a group of jumpers in on a detail from Alaska or Montana, dropped from the sky into a remote place they had never seen before, getting that sort of intelligence from a high-def camera— *you're gonna wanna angle toward the ridgetop northwest of you above the scree field for about two-thirds of a mile, then look for a cairn at the base of a big Doug fir, and follow the trail south from there until it dumps you onto an old faint two-track road*—but the gadget fetishists who dreamed of our obsolescence never bothered to imagine that we offered more than merely a pair of eyeballs, that the palimpsest of knowledge we accrued about the country year by year might have some practical value beyond that of an adorable curio.

Keeping watch over the Gila meant having the good fortune to witness a forest that was allowed to burn more aggressively than any other in the Lower 48, for the sake of the health of the land. We had witnessed the triumphs of progressive fire management, even played a small role in them, participants in a new pyromancy that no longer viewed wildfire as a disruption of the natural order, a menace, a scourge. After most of a century of total suppression, the fire managers of the Gila National Forest had adopted a strategy that helped preserve one of the healthiest ponderosa pine ecosystems in the American West. The idea was this: let a few fires burn, when and where conditions were favorable, generally in the middle elevations of the Wilderness, away from the settled edges of the forest.

The private land outside the forest boundary was essentially a sacrifice zone to cattle grazing, denuded so thoroughly it was a study in the process of desertification. The forest's fringes had been transformed as well, also overgrazed for more than a century, crisscrossed by roads and off-road-vehicle trails, pockmarked by mines, and overgrown with unburned timber and brush. In some areas wood-cutting—for cooking, heating homes, making lumber, and smelting copper ore—had altered the forest structure, and throughout the region top predators, notably grizzly bears and Mexican gray wolves, had been the object of a relentless effort at zoöcide. Against all odds the wolves were making a tentative comeback, but the grizzlies were likely gone forever.

The heart of the upper Gila River watershed nonetheless remained a land without roads, one of the wildest places left in North America, licked by flame since at least the end of the Pleistocene, and all the more beautiful and resilient for it. Standing in the middle of McKenna Park, the place in the state of New Mexico farthest from pavement, you'd have to be lobotomized or a filthy aesthete not to sense something sublime about the country: the scent of wild earth unbroken by human tools, a pine-oak savannah that called up a primeval feeling in the blood. The whole interwoven pattern of life there flourished amid frequent low-intensity burns. It had been, and remained, a fire-adapted ecosystem. The ponderosas had the ingenious habit of dropping their lowest limbs to prevent fire climbing into their crowns, giving the forest a distinctive, open look. Nearly every living tree was blackened at its base—evidence of wildfire as catalyst to evolution.

For close to four decades, the mantra on the Gila had been that fire was good, fire was necessary, but the size and character of the burns had changed. All across the world forests were succumbing to drought, disease, and beetle infestation, not to mention logging and slash-and-burn agriculture on an industrial scale. Even in the world's first Wilderness, theoretically protected from destructive human activities, the effects of global warming were evident in a new kind of megafire. This reinforced a dispiriting fact. No place on Earth could be sealed off from the effects of human activity.

One of the penalties of an ecological education is to live alone in a world of wounds, Aldo Leopold wrote seven decades ago. An ecological education was easier to come by in the 21st century than in Leopold's time. The penalty now was not to live alone with the burden of bitter knowledge—there was plenty enough company—but to feel helpless to stanch the losses foreordained by our fouling of the atmosphere with methane and carbon dioxide: losses of habitat and species, losses of forests and ice and coral reefs. As lookouts over Leopold's original American Wilderness, we had been offered a front-row seat for some of the most photogenic expressions of the Anthropocene, namely smoke and flame. It was a bittersweet privilege, watching from above as the place we loved combusted on a scale not previously seen.

One of the peculiarities of a lookout's sinecure on the Gila is to live alone inside a wound after first watching the wound be inflicted. The Whitewater-Baldy Fire set a state record when it burned 465 square miles and forced Sara and Rázik off their mountain for most of the summer of 2012. They returned to a forest in cinders. Ráz likened the loss to a kind of psychic amputation. She kept feeling the presence of the old forest all around her, but when she reached out to touch it, she found it gone.

One year later the Silver Fire repeated the scenario for me—conflagration, evacuation—and one year after that the Signal Fire came for John's mountain, just weeks before his death. Together the fires roamed across more than 440,000 of the forest's 3.3 million acres. There wasn't much to do but marvel at the heat and smoke and what they wrought, which included the incineration of the normally moist woods of the high country: Douglas and corkbark fir, blue and Engelmann spruce. It felt naïve to hope for their return in a warming world. The climatic stability that allowed them to thrive no longer prevailed; the future of a once majestic forest, at least on the high peaks, looked to be heavy on brush.

On John's last day as a lookout, the open-ended memorial enlarged for one moment to include not just old-growth forest, but one of our predecessors, one of our tribe. It unnerved me to study John's handwriting in the logbook and absorb the fact that he had saddled his horse and ridden to his death within hours of witnessing, out his tower window, those rituals honoring the memory of Bart Mortenson. The resonance of all the little details made for a paradoxical feeling, a retroactive sense of foreboding: the loved ones of a fellow lookout bearing the man's ashes to the mountain; John's mention of that now poignant word, *honeymoon*; his honoring the memory of a man by bestowing that man's name on a fire—mere hours before the fire in his own eyes went out.

⌇⌇⌇⌇⌇⌇

ALONG WITH HIS SHOCK of silver hair that appeared never to have made acquaintance with a comb, those efferevescent blue eyes were the first thing you noticed about John. Lustrous as polished turquoise, they gave his face the look of a man who never said no to the world, although that hadn't always been the case. "It took me some time to animate my face," he had written, in a notebook discovered by Teresa after his death.

When I learned he was a Minnesotan, I tried once and only once to engage him on the subject of our land of origin, but he recoiled from my mention of it so abruptly, with a look of such dread in those normally avid eyes, that I felt as if I had poked my finger in a wound. Only later would I learn that he had been there when his best friend accidentally killed himself during the winter of their senior year of high school. The friend had been fooling around with a gun in the woods while John walked a little ways ahead. He admitted he could still see the scene as if it had happened yesterday, although forty years had passed. He remembered just as vividly his parents' reaction to the tragedy: his father picking him up at the police station afterward, not even looking at him as they drove home in silence, and his mother turning away in disgust when he walked through the door, as if he were implicated in a murder.

It was not the sort of story one dropped as an icebreaker at parties. He trusted me with it, I suspect, because I first shared with him the fact that my brother killed himself with a bullet from a semiautomatic assault rifle. Sometimes you just have a feeling about people, and from the beginning of our acquaintance I judged him the kind of man who was capable of absorbing such knowledge with sensitivity and grace. From the very beginning, in fact: I shared my brother's story with him the first time I saw him face to face, at an end-of-season gathering of lookouts in the summer of 2003.

I suppose you could say I dropped it as an icebreaker at a party. Our colleague Hedge had invited a few of us to his place at Elephant Butte for beer around the backyard fire pit. For some in attendance, including me and John, it would be our first chance to connect faces with familiar voices on the radio. That just so happened to be the day John spread a first handful of Miquette's ashes in the clearing near his tower. He knew he was going to spend time with other lookouts that evening. Although he hadn't met us all in person yet, the thought of our company gave him the courage to do a thing he had been putting off for months. Within an hour of our having shaken hands that night at Hedge's, we were sharing tears over the losses of people we had loved. We began our friendship in mutual candor; it would have felt phony to proceed any other way thereafter.

Shared some time later, his story of having been a witness to his friend's death by gunshot revealed that we were blood brothers of a sort. The more we spoke of it, the more we came to understand that each of us, in the wake of a bullet's destruction, had checked into the guilt suite at the Hotel Sorrow and re-upped for a few hundred weeks, he at the age of seventeen, I at twenty-three. We had both been gnawed on by the what-if game for years and years, the sense that we could have—should have—done something to prevent a tragedy.

Nothing anyone ever told me did more to ease my loneliness, that peculiar solitude of the person who has put himself on trial, acted as judge and jury, found himself guilty of a crime of neglect, and imposed a sentence that denies the possibility of a parole into happiness. I couldn't claim John as my closest friend, nor my oldest friend, but I did find in him a man I could tell anything and be met with a voice of understanding and compassion. He never flinched or turned away, always embraced whatever I offered of myself.

That sort of human doesn't come around often.

I reviewed my life and it was also a river, Herman Hesse wrote, in the voice of Siddhartha, a line that stayed with me through the years. Whenever I recalled it, I felt an impulse to revise it for my own purposes and replace the word river with the word fire: *I reviewed my life and it was also a fire.* In fact my life was more like a series of fires, each of which moved through similar phases, from a thunderous moment of ignition—the lightning strike of a brother's suicide, the incendiary dissolution of a marriage—to the full flaring heat of grief, followed by a long, slow cooling, a landscape of ashen remains, and out of the ashes purgation and rebirth. It occurred to me more than once to share my plagiarized sentiment with John, including him in it—*I reviewed our lives and they were also fires*—but I never had, and now I never would. This thought was merely one of many that reinforced the knowledge that I had erred in assuming tomorrow remained an ongoing possibility for that combination of elements, forged in friendship, known as *us*. For me, tomorrow might still come. For him, and for us, there would be no such thing.

After our initial disclosures around the fire pit at Hedge's place, we gleefully abandoned the stilted gestures of emotional reticence that were our birthright as sons of the upper Midwest: manly handshakes, murmured small talk about the weather. With John it was all hugs, naked honesty, and lots of probing questions—real mountain man stuff, no doubt about it. *How's your soul?* I asked him once, and the question so delighted him that ever after he would ask it of me within minutes of any encounter—and he didn't let go until he got a truthful answer. His dogged curiosity could sometimes feel borderline aggressive, tenacious as a prosecutor's, even downright rude. It was as if the Catholic ritual of confession with which we had both grown up—although neither of us still practiced it formally—had morphed, with him, into a hunger for the confessions of others. He had a hard time taking no comment for an answer. Most of the time he couldn't believe you meant it. He held to the conviction that if only he pressed hard enough, you'd yield and feel better for the sharing. At the same time he had a capacity for empathy that surpassed any male of the species I had known. Our revelations of our unguarded selves sometimes brought to mind something I had read in Rilke, from his *Letters to a Young Poet*:

Do not believe that he who seeks to comfort you lives untroubled amid the simple and quiet words that sometimes do you good. His life has much difficulty and sadness and remains far behind yours. Were it otherwise, he never would have been able to find those words.

SHORTLY AFTER the fatal gunshot, John left the Minneapolis exurbs and began a life of restless movement that took him across the country and around the world, including a year-long trip through Mexico and South America, and a stint of expatriate living in Spain. His work life made for the most exotic résumé I had ever encountered: bartender, gentleman rancher, private investigator, claims adjuster for Lloyds of London, PR man and pit-crew member for an IndyCar racing team. He liked to tinker with things and once patented an invention for an elegant window blind. At the time of his death, he was president and part owner of an airplane repair business. But the job he loved to reminisce about involved his misadventures as a deputy marshal in Telluride, Colorado, where he and his boss—committed to gentler forms of justice than the code books called for—adopted the motto: *better busted by us than the real guys.*

Over time he surrounded himself with all the trappings of old-school machismo, the whole suite of midlife-crisis totems—airplane, Jeep, motorcycle, Pantera sportscar, GT40 race car—even as he cultivated his inner Midwestern penny-pincher, an archetype partial to torn blue jeans and thrift-store sweatshirts, and liable to haggle over the cost of just about anything. He liked to fly high and drive fast. He also liked sitting in one place for months, staring out the window, watching light on mountains. He lived in a house of 400 square feet with a loft bedroom but also owned a forty-foot mobile home he liked to call his "land yacht." Just when you thought you had him figured out, he showed you another facet that complicated the picture. Hermit, adventurer, homebody, horseman, life of the party and possessor of offshore investment accounts: he could not be pinned down.

More than haggling for better deals, the man loved needling bureaucratic authority, especially when he thought it unjust or blinkered. Even as a lowly agency employee (pay grade GS-4), with no health insurance, no retirement benefits, and a merely seasonal appointment ("forestry technician"), he wrote long, deeply researched letters of complaint to the chief of the Forest Service about the waste of running reconnaissance flights over a piece of country already covered by the eyes of ten lookouts. *Dear Chief Tidwell,* one such missive began, *I am a fellow Forest Service employee. I work as a fire lookout... rest assured my office is nicer than yours.* After this cheeky opening he spent nine pages eviscerating the agency's rationale for using expensive, accident-prone aircraft to detect fires and guide slurry planes in a place such as the Gila Wilderness, supposedly protected from violation by all things motorized and mechanized. His objections encompassed both the practical (wasteful spending of tax dollars, leaded-gas emissions over the forest, a history of fatal crashes of agency aircraft) and the philosophical, the latter grounded in the knowledge that the landscape we loved and claimed as part-owners, along with the rest of the American public, had been seized from the Apache in a genocidal war. Firefighting—with helicopters, slurry bombers, and paratrooper smokejumpers—was simply a way of perpetuating the endless war on the land by other means.

He nonetheless remained on a friendly, first-name basis with the aviation officers of the Gila, who always said hello via the air-to-ground frequency when they flew over his mountain on their redundant recon missions. He thought their work essentially bogus and profligate, not to mention needlessly risky with human life, but that did not prevent him from liking the people who did it, nor they him. He knew fire season was on for real when the smokejumper plane waggled its wings at him as it passed by his tower on its first flight into the fire base at Grant County Airport each spring. Like the men and women in that plane, he loved to fly circles over beautiful country—and had to admit it was quite the caper for the flyboys and flygirls to have found a way to get paid for doing it.

THE EARTH WHERE JOHN was found dead had burned in his last major wildfire as a lookout. That fire started on Mother's Day, around three in the afternoon, just off the Signal Peak Road. At first John only saw topsmoke rising out of the canyon to his north, so he made a quick call to dispatch with a tentative location in order to get firefighters moving that direction pronto. Then he checked with me to see if I had eyes on the fire. Just as I reached for the binoculars, I saw a curl of smoke rise over a ridge, twenty-two miles west of my tower and just north of his. Our triangulation of azimuths confirmed the location he had offered the dispatcher: Township 16 South, Range 13 West, Section 9. According to John's anemometer reading, winds were twenty-six to thirty-two miles per hour, with gusts to forty-two, out of the northwest—which placed him directly upslope and downwind of the fire, about the worst place to be.

An engine crew had driven to his mountain that afternoon, stopping by on a patrol of roads and campgrounds in the vicinity. When the smoke first popped up, the crew members were standing in the tower, visiting with John and Teresa, so they were unusually well-positioned to respond as the initial attack force: they could see with their own eyes exactly where they needed to go. They reached the scene within fifteen minutes, by which time the fire had grown to two acres in size by making wind-driven runs uphill. The engine crew leader assumed the role of incident commander.

He performed a quick size-up and requested additional resources. He and his men began constructing a hand line on the north side of the fire, near its point of origin, where it backed downslope into the wind. Within minutes the erratic behavior of the flames upslope from them forced them to disengage and reassess. They moved instead to the west flank of the fire and started scratching new line there.

Windy conditions made dropping smokejumpers untenable, so the jumpers arrived from the aerial fire base by vehicle, hard on the heels of a hotshot crew. Together the jumpers and hotshots conducted burnout operations between the Signal Peak Road and the northern edge of the fire, intending to use the road as a firm fuel break and an anchor point for the fire line. The leading southern and eastern edges remained too dangerous to fight. Ignited in grass, the fire had quickly leapt into the timber. Once it climbed the canopy, it became a running crown fire, with flame lengths of fifty feet and more.

John and Teresa knew they could not remain in the tower. They declined the offer of a helicopter evacuation, concerned for others in greater danger than they were, people who might need a lift from the chopper if the fire turned into a monster—hikers, campers, private property owners with forest inholdings whose only path out was blocked by the fire. With the burn moving generally east, John and Teresa had a safe escape route off the west side of the mountain, down the main trail to the highway. Before they left, they turned off the propane line to the tower, parked John's vehicle in a clearing on the edge of the helicopter LZ, and loaded their packs with a few irreplaceable items, uncertain whether the tower would still be standing upon their return.

Sometime that evening the fire crested the ridge at the base of the lookout, and the heat of the flames half-melted the flamingos John had arranged as a wry gesture of suburban lawn ornamentation. The tower escaped harm as the fire paused on the top of the ridge, leaving one side of the mountain green, the other black, with malformed pink plastic birds marking the boundary line. I later thought of them as John's final work of art, a spontaneous collaboration between his sense of whimsy and a force of nature—a force that stalled out thanks to the arrival of a back-door cold front from the east. Only the change in weather prevented the fire from growing ten times larger than its final tally of 5,484 acres and threatening the little town of Pinos Altos down below the green side of John's mountain. Overnight the humidity rose and the temperature dropped into the twenties. More crucially, the northwest wind changed to a light east one, turning the fire back upon itself. That allowed firefighters to corral the south and east sides with hand line the second day, with help from helicopter bucket drops of water on the hot spots.

But it hadn't been purely a force of nature—no lightning had been reported in the area by lookouts for weeks, and none had appeared on lightning maps available in the dispatch office. A human hand was clearly implicated in the fire's ignition. As in all such cases, two law enforcement officers (LEOs) made a pyro-forensics investigation, searching for evidence as to the cause and responsible party. The prevailing assumption among the general public is that a wildfire erases evidence of itself. On the contrary, it tends to create it—if you know how to look.

The forest LEOs arrived on scene within half an hour of John's smoke report. The incident commander showed them the two-acre area he had encountered on first contact with the fire. The LEOs marked the area and departed so as not to get in the way of the suppression effort. They spent the rest of the afternoon patrolling the general vicinity in search of anyone who might have seen something suspicious.

On the following afternoon, the crew chief and the two LEOs walked the original two-acre perimeter, first clockwise, then counter-clockwise. They did so with an eye to fire-direction indicators they could trace toward the specific point of origin. Something as simple as the shape of a burned oak leaf, for instance, could offer a clue; typically green leaves curl in such a way that they point toward oncoming heat. The angle of the char on standing tree trunks provides another clue. Advancing fire—pushed by wind or moving upslope—will leave a line of char on trees at a higher angle than the angle of the slope, with the low side indicating the direction from which the fire came. Backing fire—that is, fire moving into the wind, or down a slope—will leave char on a line parallel to the ground all around the tree trunk. In grass, advancing fire burns all but the very base of the stem, while backing fire consumes the base so that some stems fall unburned, the seed heads generally pointing in the direction from which the fire came. Finally, in low-intensity fire—often close to the source of ignition—signs of "protection" will be visible, meaning fire will burn only one side of a tree trunk or fallen log. When looking at the protected, unburned sides, a human faces the origin of the fire.

By following these directional indicators backwards, reversing the path of the fire's movement, the LEOs eventually focused on a ten-by-ten-foot patch of disturbed ground that represented a transition zone where backing and advancing fire converged: the point of origin. The fire appeared to have started in or near a burnt stump. The LEOs found two bullets inside the remains of the stump, and next to it an empty one-ounce bottle of Fireball liquor and two cigarette butts. Because they could not determine the precise place where an ignition source first came into contact with flammable material, they never named an official cause. It may have been residual heat from the bullets in the stump hole, assuming they had just been fired. It may have been one of the cigarettes or a match used to light it. It may have been some other ignition source that the guilty party was smart enough not to leave behind.

Several possible witnesses were interviewed in the ten days following the fire, and despite tantalizing clues—there was more than one mention of a light-colored SUV in the area around the time the smoke first boiled up—the person or persons responsible never faced any consequences.

TWELVE DAYS AFTER fleeing his mountain, John had returned and resumed lookout duties when three students from Silver City flew over his tower in a private plane. Their charter high school, named in honor of Aldo Leopold, emphasized outdoor education and experiential learning, and it took seriously Leopold's proposition that Wilderness could serve as "a laboratory for the study of land-health." With that idea to guide their efforts, the students monitored soil conditions in a recent burn scar, tested water quality on the Gila River and its three headwater forks, and kept watch over more than a dozen study transects in the forest, tracking vegetation changes. One of those transects—number seven—just so happened to run along the north slope of Signal

Peak. Now it had burned, which only amplified the importance of their work. They were eager to have a look at the changes.

Two of the kids were sixteen years old, the other fourteen. All were sophomores and members of the school's Envirothon team, which competed in an annual statewide science contest. Their team, in fact, had won the state championship six weeks earlier. The boy among them, Michael Mahl, had just been selected student body president for the next year—the youngest ever at the school—in an election that was uncontested because everyone knew he would win. Blond-haired and blue-eyed, he possessed an impressive collection of cheap sunglasses that often hid those eyes behind a mirrored surface. He loved playing "The Legend of Zelda" video game series, which helped him overcome his early struggles with reading. A dedicated musician, he taught himself to play a didgeridoo he had fashioned from a yucca stalk with his own two hands. He performed most Sundays with his family at a church in Silver City led by his pastor grandfather. In addition to his major passion for the guitar, he played drums, ukulele, and mandolin.

Ella Sala Myers rode her horse Gracie six days a week—a big Dutch mare with a spirit to match her size—and wrote two novels before she earned a driver's license. Tall and fair-skinned, she had the dignified posture of a trained equestrian competitor, with specialties in jumping horses and dressage. She played the violin and fiddle and took beautiful, almost abstract photographs of clouds from the back door of her family's home. She had just been awarded a scholarship for a summer course at the Art Institute of Chicago on the basis of a short movie she had shot and directed herself. I once shared dinner with her and her family and some mutual friends at a Mexican restaurant in Silver City, during which the two of us traded stories of our writing endeavors. At the time we had each written one book, though she was twenty-six years younger than me. Hers won a Regional Scholastic Arts Award, but she was shy about it. Her older sister Raven, like a diligent publicist, kept nudging her to go on and say more whenever she appeared on the verge of clamming up.

Ella Jaz Kirk, the youngest of the three, had an easy grace earned by dancing ballet from a young age. Brown-eyed and willowy, with a long mane of dark hair spilling past her shoulders, she too had an aptitude for music. She wrote poetry and songs and, accompanied by her mother and several friends, recorded her first studio album when she was twelve, playing the fiddle and singing lead vocals. When the Interstate Stream Commission in Santa Fe began making serious noises about destroying the Gila River with a diversion dam, she set to work collecting more than 6,400 signatures on her self-authored petition to protect the river's free-flowing beauty, making of her own voice a megaphone she shared with others. She delivered her petition to the governor and testified about the issue before a state legislative committee with the poise of someone thrice her age, an act that inspired the community of conservationists around Silver City.

The three students were more than colleagues, they were good friends. The Ellas played fiddle together in a group that sometimes got together to make music, and unbeknownst to the rest of the world, Ella Jaz and Michael Mahl had recently admitted their mutual attraction and held hands while watching a thunderstorm play on the horizon. Normally eco-monitor work called for a team leader, but they respected each other too much to elevate one above the others. Together they decided that Ella Myers was the soul, Ella Jaz the voice, and Michael Mahl the heart of their trio, and they chose an egalitarian approach to their work by which each of them took the lead on one aspect—Michael Mahl soils, Ella Jaz the watershed, Ella Myers forestry. At so tender an age, they already knew the truth of a line from the poet Mary Oliver: *Attention is the beginning of devotion.*

As the forestry leader, it fell to Ella Myers to make inquiries with the Forest Service about getting a look at their transect. She first sought permission to drive in on the Signal Peak Road, a request the Forest Service denied due to the hazard of falling trees in the burn scar. The area remained closed to the public—closed to everyone but John and our USFS colleagues. Aware, then, that the only way to see the transect was from the air, she asked whether she and her fellow students might ride along on a Forest Service reconnaissance flight. The agency rejected that request too, for liability reasons.

On the very last day of teacher meetings for the school year, three days after classes had ended for the students, an unexpected opportunity arose. That morning Steve Blake—the science teacher who oversaw their eco-monitoring projects and coached their Envirothon team—had an idea. He learned from his wife Denise that her first task of the day was to pick up a doctor she worked with at the Veterans Affairs health clinic in Silver City. Every other Friday Peter Hochla flew in his own private plane from his home base in Albuquerque to Whiskey Creek Airport, in Silver City, in order to treat psychiatric patients at the VA. He did the same at numerous other clinics around New Mexico, flying somewhere almost every weekday. He had arranged his professional life around the project of serving underserved veterans in the rural parts of a poor state. Now and then one of his far-flung patients required emergency transfer to the VA in Albuquerque. When that happened he would personally offer to fly family members in if they couldn't afford to travel to be with their loved one— another sort of air-angel impulse.

On days when he flew to Silver City, Denise Blake often met him at the airport and drove him the final ten minutes of his journey to work. More than once Dr. Hochla had offered to take the Blakes along on his flight back to Albuquerque, if they ever had reason to travel there. Although they had never taken him up on the offer, it now occurred to Steve Blake to wonder whether the doctor might be willing to make a quick jaunt over the Signal Fire scar before flying home that day, as a favor to him and his students. A beloved educator, the most popular teacher at the school and, in the words of a colleague, a "brilliant maverick," Steve Blake was always on the lookout for ways to give his students exciting learning experiences. He knew time had almost run out ahead of summer break, when the kids would scatter, and here was a devoted caregiver with an airplane and a generous disposition.

"Do you think there's any way that he would consider taking the eco-monitors over the burn site?" Steve Blake asked his wife Denise.

She said she would put the question to him when she picked him up at the airport.

"It sounds like a worthy project," Dr. Hochla said, when Denise brought it up. "I need to think about it."

BY LUNCHTIME, having had a chance to mull over Blake's request and ask a few questions about the nature of the students' project, Dr. Hochla indicated he was inclined to say yes. He cautioned that the students shouldn't count on it, because he had a personal policy of never flying in bad weather. If he saw lightning in the area ahead of time, he would have to call off the flight. Meanwhile he would need permission slips signed by the parents, in the event the weather cooperated.

Tied up in meetings at the school, Blake didn't have a chance to discuss the idea with his students in person. Instead he sent them a text message, alerting them to the potential of a flight over their transect, and urging them to procure permission slips from their parents if they wanted to go. He told them not to get too excited—it wasn't a sure thing—but to be prepared in case it came off as planned.

I have something at 6, Ella Jaz texted back. *How long would this take? Do you think we'll be done by 6?*

Planes don't stop at stoplights, Blake replied.

THE STUDENTS HAD intended to be at the school that afternoon to wrap up work on a Youth Conservation Corps grant application for the coming year, so it was no inconvenience to meet up with Blake in time for a three o'clock flight.

Ella Myers' mother, Jennifer Douglass, delivered her permission slip to the school in person and talked with Blake about the flight. He told her how the doctor flew all over the state visiting VA clinics for his work. Dr. Hochla, Blake said, never flew in bad weather—indeed he once stayed over with the Blakes when storms prevented him from returning to Albuquerque safely. If the weather looked unfavorable, the trip would have to wait.

Michael Mahl's father signed his son's permission slip and asked if there was room on the flight for one more. If so, he'd like to go along for the ride. The question was passed along to Dr. Hochla, and the answer came back no—only three empty seats and a weight limit besides.

Until that moment Blake had assumed he'd accompany his students on the flight, but now it was clear there would be room only for them.

When Ella Jaz mentioned the flight to her mother, Patrice Mutchnick called the main number at the school to inquire about the details. As the single parent of an only child, Patrice, by her own admission, took extra caution with the safety of her daughter, whose father had died when Ella Jaz was two years old. The secretary who answered the phone claimed no knowledge of the trip, so Patrice asked to speak directly with Blake. He repeated what he had told Jennifer Douglass about the doctor's experience flying around the state to rural VA clinics, about his aversion to flying in bad weather, and how the flight would be called off if they saw any lightning.

Patrice typed up and printed a permission slip in her office at Western New Mexico University, where she worked as a biology lab director. Ella Jaz rode her bike across town to pick it up. The two of them talked about the flight and the possibility it might not happen.

"I'm concerned that the weather could deteriorate," Patrice said.

"Don't project your fears," Ella Jaz said. "I'm not afraid to fly."

"Well, I'm not afraid of flying, but if the weather gets bad, you are not going to fly."

"Don't worry," Ella Jaz said, "everything's going to be okay."

LESS THAN TWO HOURS LATER, Patrice sat in her office looking at real-time radar and a lightning-map indicator that showed the first ground strikes of the day in the vicinity of Signal Peak. As an educator and experienced group leader for outdoor adventure trips involving children, her unease had increased in the time since Ella Jaz pedaled off with her permission slip. She didn't like the look of the weather—it was a repeat of the day before, when there had been erratic winds and dry lightning, followed by a brief hard rain.

She left her office and went outside to look at the sky. She sent a text message to Blake: *Radar. Lightning just north. Rain just west. Feeling drops now.*

Thanks, he wrote in response. *We haven't left for airport yet.*

Check radar, she replied.

Will do and show Peter if he hasn't already.

AT THE VA CLINIC, Dr. Hochla learned he had a patient in need of an emergency consultation, so the meeting time for the flight got pushed back to 3:15.

The students used the extra time to finalize their YCC grant application for the coming year, which would fund their eco-monitor efforts as a paid internship. They chose the fellow students they would mentor on their soil, water, and forest projects, once classes resumed in the fall. They filled every inch of the whiteboard in Blake's classroom with their ideas. They felt pleased to be tying up their last loose ends for the school year and giddy about the flight to come. Just after 3:00 they climbed into Michael Mahl's truck in the school parking lot and headed for the airport along Highway 180, a drive of four and a half miles. Ella Jaz called her mother on the way.

"We're headed to the airport, Mom," she said.

"You're probably not going to fly," Patrice said, "so don't be disappointed if you get out there and you don't fly."

"Okay, Mom," Ella Jaz said.

"Maybe you'll just meet the pilot and you'll find another day," Patrice said. "So call me if you are going to get on the plane."

"Okay, Mom. Love you."

WHEN EVERYONE INVOLVED met at the airport—the kids arriving in Michael Mahl's pickup truck, Steve Blake in his own vehicle, Dr. Hochla and Denise Blake in hers—Steve Blake introduced the kids to Dr. Hochla. "Thanks a lot for offering to do this," Blake said. "It's very nice of you."

Blake raised the subject of the weather. He mentioned the link to local radar he had received from Patrice, but Dr. Hochla waved him off. "The radar that you get on your apps is not the radar that matters to me," Dr. Hochla said. Like many pilots, he used a program that offered 3-D displays of icing, turbulence, winds, temperature, and humidity, both in horizontal and vertical views, at specific flight elevations.

Blake pointed out storm cells visible to the south and west and asked if they were a concern. "We'll be there and back before that's a problem," Dr. Hochla said. It was a trip of less than ten miles one way, a simple out and back that would have them on the ground again in fifteen or twenty minutes.

Dr. Hochla put his briefcase and landing-gear chock blocks in Denise Blake's car. While he went through his preflight safety checklist, the students posed for pictures next to the plane. Ella Jaz took several of the shiny propeller and nose cone, to show her mother how clean and well-maintained the Beechcraft Bonanza was.

When it came time to climb aboard, the students bantered over who ought to get the front passenger's seat. Michael and

Ella Jaz teased each other—Michael insisted they flip a coin for the privilege. Ella Jaz beat Michael Mahl on the first flip. Ella Myers won her flip with Ella Jaz. Michael pointed out that for the game to be fair and square, Ella Myers had to beat him too, so they flipped again. Ella Myers won. To Blake, standing there watching his prize students—the best he had ever had in more than two decades of teaching, he thought—the result had a certain satisfaction to it. Ella Myers led the group's forestry work. She ought to be the one to sit up front.

"Steve, you're getting on the plane, aren't you?" Ella Jaz said.

"No. There's no room."

"Well, just come on," she teased. "There's room in the back."

"You don't want an extra 185 pounds weighing you down," he said.

He told them not to worry about taking good pictures of the burn scar. "The most important thing is to get Aldo Leopold's view," he said, "the big-picture view."

Dr. Hochla climbed aboard through the right-side door, into the left-side pilot's seat. Ella Myers climbed aboard after him—but not before giving Blake a goodbye hug.

"Have a great time," he told her.

MEANWHILE, IN HER OFFICE AT WNMU, Patrice felt increasingly fidgety and scared. The weather had continued to deteriorate. The wind had picked up noticeably. Sailors speak of rogue waves on the open ocean, but in Silver City that day, in places all over town, people later remembered the rogue winds. They seemed to come out of nowhere, blowing down signs, slamming car doors, creating dust devils.

Patrice hadn't heard back from Ella Jaz or Steve Blake about the status of the flight. She sent Blake a text message.

I'm anxious, she wrote. *Please pick better flying weather.*

He did not respond.

ELLA, ELLA JAZ, AND MICHAEL donned headsets and secured their seat belts. Dr. Hochla gave them final instructions, then taxied from the ramp onto the runway. The airport wind sock showed a breeze out of the west at ten to fifteen knots, with an occasional gust at twenty. The plane hesitated for a minute while the Blakes watched. Then it accelerated into the wind and rose into the sky. It was 3:36 p.m.

Around 3:40 or a little after, still having heard nothing from either Steve Blake or Ella Jaz, Patrice dialed Blake's number.

"Steve, what the hell is going on?" she asked.

"They're on their way back," he said.

"What the hell are you talking about? What do you mean?" She had expected a call from Ella Jaz if the flight was still on.

"Well, they took off a little while ago. They're on their way back."

"Why aren't you on the plane?"

He explained that although he had planned to join the kids on the flight, it turned out there wasn't room for four passengers, only three, so he had stayed behind. Patrice couldn't believe he hadn't gone along as their mentor and chaperone. She expressed her displeasure in no uncertain terms.

During their conversation, Blake's phone registered the arrival of a text message.

It was the one Patrice had sent fifteen minutes earlier, delayed somehow en route.

I'm anxious. Please pick better flying weather.

DR. HOCHLA FLEW NORTH toward Signal Peak, approached the mountain from the west, and did a clockwise loop around the north slope, during which the kids took video and photos of the burn scar. It was a fantastic view out the window over the right wing, the whole fire visible below them in black, their vantage like that of a bird's.

From his tower, John heard the plane approaching. He grabbed his binoculars, stepped onto the catwalk, sighted in, and reported to dispatch the presence of the single-engine aircraft, in keeping with lookout protocol. All of us did the same when low-flying planes came within earshot, our reports a courtesy and safety precaution aimed at our own agency aircraft, so there would be no surprises in their airspace.

The dispatcher acknowledged his report and thanked him, as was also customary.

The plane turned south, headed back to Whiskey Creek.

ON THE PHONE, Blake told Patrice the kids should be back any minute. "I'll call you as soon as I see the plane," he said.

When he hung up, unnerved by Patrice's agitation at his not having gone along on the flight—not to mention her late-arriving text—he began shaking with fear.

"Call Peter and tell him to come back," he told his wife, "because Patrice is not happy."

Denise Blake dialed Dr. Hochla's cell phone.

Busy piloting the plane, he did not answer.

TOO AGITATED TO WAIT for a call back, Patrice got in her car and drove toward the high school, intending to meet Ella Jaz when she returned from Whiskey Creek. At the last moment before the turn to the school, gripped by a disturbing premonition—"a horribly scary feeling" as she later described it—she chose instead to continue on the highway to the airport.

DR. HOCHLA MADE HIS APPROACH for landing on the north-south runway from the west. The wind had picked up since his takeoff fifteen minutes earlier, steady at fifteen knots, with gusts to twenty-five, out of the west. The tailwind caused him to come in at a high rate of speed. He carried past the runway centerline as he banked left on final turn for landing. The plane required sixty degrees of bank, the left wing tipped low, to realign with the runway. Dr. Hochla now had to battle a crosswind and still hadn't touched down with more than half the runway already behind him. A man in one of the hangars who heard the approach and stepped outside to watch shouted, "Go around, go around!"—urging the plane to abort the landing, stay aloft, and circle back for another attempt.

A few seconds later the wheels touched down.

GPS DATA SHOWED that landing occurred at 3:52 p.m. and 53 seconds. The plane's speed was 120 knots. The high speed and angle of approach caused the plane to bounce. It remained aloft for three seconds before the wheels touched down again. Its speed was now 100 knots. Roughly 1,800 feet of runway remained, or slightly more than one-third of its total length of just under a mile. The plane remained on the runway for approximately 750 feet. Its speed decreased to 87 knots. With a little more than 1,000 feet of runway remaining, Dr. Hochla must have seen that the plane would not stop before the end. It would be a bumpy ride on the overrun, and his tires would likely be damaged.

Instead of applying the brakes and enduring the white-knuckle ride off the runway, he chose to apply power and attempt a go-around.

THE SHOUT OF "GO AROUND, GO AROUND!" caught the attention of a pilot working on a hundred-hour inspection of his own aircraft inside the Whiskey Creek maintenance hangar. He later wrote of what he witnessed:

I was only a few feet from the door so I stepped outside to see what was going on. I saw the Doc's plane having a real time of it trying to get back onto the runway. At this point he had used up 75% of the runway. The aircraft was finally down on all three wheels… My thought was that he would really be burning up the tires trying to stop at that point, but might make it by the end with a high possibility of over-run.

There was an approximate three-second hesitation, and then a go-around power was applied at that time. With less than 20% of runway left, I saw no way for that to work. I ran to the center of my ramp to see him rotate at the end of the runway, with no real climb rate. The aircraft went straight ahead for approximately 1/4 mile and sank out of sight, then rose again to original rotation altitude. I said out loud, "I think he might make it." The landing gear was never raised to the up-position that I could see. Then he turned to the east at approximately 20 degree bank, into approximately 15 knots, gusting to 20 knot tail wind. At that point, I told my nephew to call 911.

FROM HIS VANTAGE on Signal Peak, John reported a new smoke near the landing strip at Whiskey Creek, aware of what it meant from the moment he spotted it. *Aircraft down in Silver City,* I copied in my logbook, recording John's report to the dispatcher. *Township 17 South, Range 13 West, Section 32. Has started a fire in residential area off Flury Lane.*

PATRICE CRESTED THE HILL on the highway next to the Walmart superstore, where the view opened out to the east over the area surrounding the airport. Below her, about three miles distant, she saw a plume of smoke.

She knew what it meant.

AT THE TRACTOR SUPPLY STORE next to the Walmart, Ella Myers' mother, Jennifer Douglass, and Ella's sister, Raven, emerged from an errand into the parking lot. They looked east and saw smoke.

They feared what it meant.

AT HIS FAMILY'S SIGN-MAKING BUSINESS, two miles from the airport, John Mahl heard siren after siren pass by on the highway. He logged onto social media to ask if anyone knew what had happened to cause the commotion. The first response: a plane had crashed near Whiskey Creek.

He had no doubt what it meant.

IN MY TOWER, unable to see the smoke due to storm clouds, I copied into my logbook the radio chatter I overheard in the next hour.

> *15:59 — Air Attack 96 Golf over scene of crash*
> *16:05 — One structure on fire, active ground fire in the grass at crash site*
> *16:30 — Fire at crash site under control*

At 18:00 I logged out of service, went for an evening walk, and thought no more of it.

IN OUR LINE OF WORK, it is forbidden to discuss injuries or fatalities in any detail over government radios, for the sake of the privacy of those involved. Lacking access to the social grapevine of friends and neighbors, or even to a local newspaper, I would go another six days before learning the identities of the crash victims. During that time, alone on my mountain, it never occurred to me I might know them—in part because the only pilot of my acquaintance was John.

As he would have known, landing an airplane is a long, unfolding process that begins many miles before the runway. The main goal is what is known in the flying world as a "stabilized approach." Several factors comprise the choreography of landing. Airspeed must be controlled, rate of descent calibrated, power setting managed, wind corrected for. Each influences the others, and together they must be integrated to achieve touchdown in the proper landing zone of the runway.

The National Transportation Safety Board report on the crash would make clear that Dr. Hochla failed to manage this choreography. His base approach—the penultimate leg of the flight, conducted at a right angle to the runway—occurred at too high a rate of speed. He struggled in his efforts to correct for the gusty tailwind, which became a crosswind once he made his final turn. A bank angle of thirty degrees or less meets the Federal Aviation Administration's criteria for a stabilized approach on final turn for landing. Dr. Hochla banked at twice that in an effort to align over the runway. Wind of more than seventeen knots exceeds the maximum crosswind limit for the Beechcraft Bonanza, as published in the Pilot's Operating Handbook. Multiple reports from eyewitnesses, as well as measured gusts nearby, noted wind at twenty-five knots at the time of landing.

His excess speed, his struggles with wind, his extreme bank angle—each and every one of these, never mind all of them together, called for a go-around, just as the witness in the hangar urged, in a shout Dr. Hochla could not hear.

By going around—in other words, aborting the landing and staying airborne to circle back for another attempt—Dr. Hochla would have increased his options for a safe touchdown. He could have chosen to fly his base approach over a greater distance the second time, giving himself more room to make adjustments for wind, more time to manage his speed. Or he could have chosen to skip landing at Whiskey Creek and instead fly less than ten miles south to Grant County Airport, where the runway was situated on an east-west axis instead of a north-south one. That would have offered a more desirable final approach into a headwind.

Dr. Hochla had accrued more than 3,600 hours of flight time. His pilot log showed that he had made the decision to abort a landing and go around more than once in the past, when conditions dictated that as the safer alternative. It is a routine act, performed eventually by any pilot who flies long enough, and a mandatory part of flight training. Why he didn't do it this time, we can only speculate.

The most convincing argument I would encounter came a year and a half later, when I read a report on the crash by a man named Don Lewis. A commercial airline pilot with more than 20,000 hours of flight experience, he studied all the available evidence to hazard some theories about the crucial last seconds of the flight, at the behest of the students' families and their lawyers. For him, two theories of human behavior provided a conceptual framework for explaining the crash: "normalization of deviance" and "mission completion bias."

Normalization of deviance proposes that, in Lewis's words, *it worked out in the past so it will work out again, in spite of being incorrect.* He went on: *I believe that* [Dr. Hochla] *had become comfortable with the Bonanza and was accustomed to it stopping when he finally touched down. But the problem is, if the landing zone is not the goal then what is? The last time it stopped after landing halfway down the runway. Surely it will stop if I go a little beyond that, or a little beyond that; and so on and so forth. Eventually such a normalization of deviance leads to an incident unless it is recognized and stopped...*

Lewis studied Dr. Hochla's pilot logbook and found mention of more than one anomalous landing. *On 25 February 2004 there is a note about having a propeller strike during a crosswind landing,* Lewis wrote. *Having a propeller strike on landing is the result of approaching the runway at excessive speed and trying to force the aircraft onto the runway. After this event the incident pilot seemed very diligent to highlight flights that included crosswind landings or strong winds in the remarks section of his logbook... In 2006 on 15 March and 9 May the pilot commented on diverting to alternate airports due to high crosswinds at the airport of intended landing. There were also mentions of go-arounds both during training and non-training flights. All examples of good aeronautical decision-making and judgment.*

On 5 February 2010 the pilot mentioned blowing a tire on landing at Whiskey Creek Airport. While this could have been a defect with that particular tire, it was more likely not. This is representative of a landing that was too fast or too long requiring heavy braking to stop the airplane on the remaining runway...

Flying is such a multi-faceted and complex endeavor that it is not uncommon to have a weakness in one area. I believe the incident pilot's weakness was landing the airplane in gusty conditions. I believe that under any other circumstance the pilot would likely have gone around or even diverted to another airport; he had exhibited this decision-making in the past... Unfortunately once a pilot starts operating outside of normal boundaries then there remains no guidepost whereby to recognize boundaries.

The key words in that passage, *under any other circumstance,* lead us to the second half of Lewis' two-part conceptual framework: the theory of mission completion bias. As articulated by Lewis, it proposes that when a conscientious person feels an unusual urgency to complete a task, that urgency can alter his decision-making process in adverse ways. *This was not a routine flight for him, this was a special flight; a sightseeing flight for children,* Lewis wrote. *It is my opinion that he felt pressure to conclude the mission as promised to the concerned parents and teachers waiting back on the ground. This concept is not at all rare, and is in fact one of the many external pressures that pilots are cautioned against.*

Another way to say it is that the laws of gravity and physics do not change because a plane carries special passengers—in this case, other people's kids—but a pilot's thinking might be affected if he's not careful, the self-imposed pressure to complete the mission overriding his training and experience.

If Lewis was right, it was Dr. Hochla's urgently felt desire to get the students safely back on the ground that caused him, in an excruciating irony, to do just the opposite.

THE WEEK FOLLOWING THE CRASH, when I cruised into Silver City for my days off, I found a community wounded and bewildered, and an ongoing process of commemoration about which I had known nothing. Having buried a brother gone far too young, I had more than an inkling of what those closest to the dead were feeling. Some of them felt an understandable wish to be gone themselves. Patrice, with whom I had friends in common, was in the care of people who took the precaution of removing the knives and pills from her home. She had been one of the first people on scene at the crash, and it seared images in her memory that would haunt her for years. Steve Blake, with whom I also had friends in common, was on a twenty-four-hour suicide watch, heavily medicated and practically catatonic, speaking only to say, over and over, that he wished he had been on the plane. He would teach one more year at the school before retiring, unable to continue working with kids.

If I had acted as a proper citizen of my community, I would have participated in the public process of mourning the dead. It would have been entirely natural to join the collective effort of making meaning from their brief, passionate lives. But coming off my mountain to belatedly enter the circle of grief felt awkward in a way I couldn't quite pinpoint in the moment. The best I can surmise is that for the first time in a dozen years I felt disadvantaged by the solitude of my vocation. I could not assimilate the facts of the matter into my reality. I could not accept the absence from the world of those kids. Not long before I had sat in the same classroom with Ella Myers and Ella Jaz, both of them participants in a writing workshop I conducted for their English class. Even more recently I had sat at the bar in Silver City's finest public gathering place, Diane's Parlor, and listened to Michael Mahl sing and play acoustic guitar at an open-mic event. To think of them gone forever, their voices silenced, was both appalling and preposterous.

Reality being insistent, I became at first discombobulated, then angry. Instead of recognizing my anger and confusion for the selfish impulses they were, I used them as a shield to deflect my attention from the loss of those three beautiful human beings already well along a path of artistry and civic engagement, not to mention the pilot who had volunteered his time to enrich their education.

A thousand people attended the kids' memorial service in Silver City, but I was not among them. Nor was I there when Patrice gathered with friends to scatter some of Ella Jaz's ashes in the river near the headwaters confluence, everyone swimming together with them, laughing and crying amid the ashes' swirl and flow. My work having granted me a certain remove from the immediate shock of the crash, I resolved to maintain my stance apart. I would find some private means of honoring their lives.

That aloof and contorted pose would last another two weeks, until news of John's accident reached me through a telephone.

If I had wanted distance from death, death had other ideas.

BIRTHDAY FOR THE NEXT FOREST

BY SHEER DUMB LUCK I happened to be facing the lightning when it struck: a livid filament that reappeared on my eyelids when I blinked. A blue puff of smoke bloomed skyward from the top of the ridge, superheated sap boiled to vapor in an instant. It dispersed on the breeze so quickly I wondered whether I had imagined it—whether, having become at last clinically pyromaniacal, I had willed the tree to catch fire and conjured the evidence to prove it.

I reached for the field glasses where they hung from a hook in the ceiling of the tower, an instinctual move made without looking away from the spot of the strike. I lifted the binoculars to my eyes, focused on the ridge line. Waited. Remembered to breathe. Waited some more. Nothing amiss. Nothing new or different along the contour of the hill.

Then it happened: the slightest rupture in the continuity of the view, a light white fog that ghosted the length of the tree and twisted through its branches, only to disperse again on the breeze. This smudge of smoke confirmed that I hadn't been hallucinating—that indeed a bolt from the clouds had lit the tree on fire, and I had been witness to the genesis. I set the binoculars aside, crouched behind the peephole of my Osborne Fire Finder, and waited for the smoke to puff again. When it did, I aimed the crosshairs through the viewfinder and noted the azimuth to the fraction of a degree.

This fact in hand, I turned to my maps and compared what they told me with the topography surrounding the smoke, noting its relation to the nearest prominent feature on the landscape, a small but unmistakable peak. Confident I had pinned the fire within a single square mile on the map, I called the dispatcher with my report: lightning-struck snag, narrow column of light-colored smoke, compass direction from me expressed in degrees azimuth, location by township, range, and section. The Silver Fire: named for nearby Silver Creek.

This one appeared poised to go big and stay awhile.

The conditions of the forest where it occurred foretold what the fire became; or as we say in the business, fuel structure aligned with weather to offer high spread potential. All the ingredients for a conflagration were in place. For the sake of cattle forage and stability on the watershed and a pleasing view of dense green trees from a tourist highway and a dozen other excuses that taken together amounted to outmoded and contradictory dogma, the surrounding country had been starved of fire—every new smoke suppressed as quickly as possible—going back a hundred years, an astonishing feat of military technology and human hubris. The result was an overgrown, unhealthy patch of forest further stressed by the realities of climate change. Thousands of dead white fir trees, killed by beetles a decade earlier, sprinkled the surrounding hillsides, and fuel moisture in the living trees had been sapped by years of substandard snow pack and above-average temperatures.

The weather forecast predicted the trifecta of hot, dry, windy conditions in the days ahead. All available smokejumpers had been dropped on two other fires earlier in the afternoon, so none were still on call for initial attack. Despite being well outside the Wilderness, the topography was too steep and thickly forested for helicopter landings, so the only option for suppression was to send an engine crew whose members would have to hike cross country from the end of a bad dirt road, a trip that took four hours, drive time included.

For two full days I had a grandstand seat as my colleagues performed their suppression efforts—first the ground crew scratching a containment line around the fire, then air tankers dropping fire-retardant slurry from above. The containment line didn't hold because big conifers kept toppling and rolling downslope, starting new spot fires below the crew, who had no choice but to flee for their lives. I stayed in service with them past midnight that first night, scanning their radio traffic on the tactical channel, eavesdropping on their progress and offering a communication link if they needed one, but I was of no use to their doomed efforts.

The next day's repeated slurry drops didn't hold because the fire had grown too hot, actively burning through the sundown hours when agency planes were forbidden to fly for safety reasons. They offered an impressive spectacle by daylight, two alternating bombers flying low over the ridge, first one, then the other, load-and-return from the aerial fire base all day long. The red-tinted mud unfurled in translucent streamers, dispersing into the treetops like a poison mist, but every drop of it—50,000 gallons of slurry, plus another 30,000 of water—was for naught. It was one more run at the old game, putting out fires with emergency money in liquid form, but the rules of that game had been written in a previous century, under conditions that no longer applied. A hotshot crew sent to scout the country for containment strategies reported back that there were none that didn't risk injury or death.

On the fire's second night, I stood in the meadow on top of my mountain and watched the flames rupture the dark like lava spewing from a fissure in the earth. The slow-motion momentum of a natural catastrophe exerted a powerful spell: the sight menaced and titillated in equal measure. Even after I called out of service for the evening, I couldn't step away for more than half an hour before returning to the tower and staring some more. The fire had spread over seventy acres. The question now was whether the entire length of the Black Range would burn, or if some portion would be spared.

Late in the morning of day three, a running crown fire took off in the canopy as the wind pushed the flames upslope toward the crest of the range. Two hundred acres burned in the span of an hour, trees torching like Roman candles in flame lengths of 100 feet. Mesmerized, I watched the smoke—first white, then darkening through various shades of gray, finally culminating in black—rise skyward like the plume from a muddy geyser.

The order to evacuate came just after lunch. I was told I had forty-five minutes to grab the possessions dearest to me and lock up the facilities for a departure of indefinite duration. A helicopter would soon spool up to pluck me from the peak and deliver me to the trailhead, where my truck was parked directly in the path of the fire.

I hauled my gear out to the Marston Mat helipad—typewriter, box of books, backpack full of clothes, cooler of perishable food, a few other odds and ends—and made one last walk around the mountain, noting the various man-made flammables. Among them were the aspenwood hitching post I had just rebuilt, the picket fence around the propane tanks, the sign welcoming visitors, the old log cabin. Whether any or all would remain when I returned was an open question.

Oblivious to the drama playing out five miles south, hummingbirds clustered at the feeders I had hung for them. They drank my simple syrup mixture, chittering and whistling, flaring their wings to mime dominance or dislodge a seat at the table. The syrup would be gone in a day or two without me around to replenish it—but the fire would force the birds to find new feeding grounds anyway. They would move on. They would survive.

Soon the distant buzz of the chopper made itself heard, a low percussive hum that gathered strength until it roared over the meadow. The grass bent beneath the force of the rotor like seaweed swaying in the tide. Two helitack personnel ducked out the side door and loaded my supplies, a perfunctory job, performed wordlessly. It was a humbling and even sort of sickening feeling to board the machine for the flight out. More than a hundred times I had come and gone from the mountain over the years, mostly under power of my own two legs, a few times by the legs of a horse. To leave by the magic of internal combustion was as dispiriting as it was novel, almost equal parts elation and despair, with a side helping of guilt given my devotion to non-motorized Wilderness travel. The point of the work is early detection: the sooner you spot a fire, the more options you give firefighters to manage it. When you're airlifted by the whirlybird, their options have dwindled, and so have yours—to none but run.

Over the course of eleven summers, I had sat in my mountain minaret and marveled at the harshness and beauty of the view, but to see it for the first time from a bird's perspective astonished me anew. As the chopper rumbled along the crest toward the trailhead, I looked out the window upon a forbidding landscape, east-west canyons dropping sharply from the top of the divide, each of them cradled by shark-fin ridges and brutal bluffs—a forest of Douglas fir and white pine on the high peaks, pockets of aspen on the north-facing slopes, ponderosa on the south aspects, here and there a piñon pine. The smooth white bark of certain aspens still showed cowboy dendroglyphs carved almost a century ago. Amid them stood gnarly survivor trees whose bark had been corkscrewed by lightning. Others were marked by the scars of old ground fires at their base. A few of them had been almost like friends to me, sources of wonder and comfort. Their cool breath. Their proud bearing. Their highly individual shapes. Being among the most rooted of life forms—challenged by changing climatic conditions, unable to flee more immediate catastrophes—they were uniquely vulnerable organisms, which only added to their beauty. I tried to fix them in my imagination even as I bid them goodbye.

When we landed at the pass, I stepped from the chopper and removed my flight helmet to watch the smoke rise and spin like a cyclone to the south, a vortex of unimaginable heat. Ash fell like flakes of snow on the hood of my pickup truck, and the growl of the fire could be heard more than a mile away.

I joined the Black Range district ranger and three firefighters standing on the edge of the paved overlook, none of us quite capable of articulating the awe we felt at what we saw and what it meant for a forest we knew well and loved. I reminded myself that the mountains had always known fire, were in fact born in a cataclysm of fire, during a great volcanic explosion in the Eocene Epoch, an event orders of magnitude more dazzling than even the most spectacular wildfire.

Created in fire, the mountains would naturally succumb to it for renewal and rebirth. June 7, 2013, happened to be the day they did so.

WHEN I FIRST BECAME A LOOKOUT, during the fire season of 2002, I was as green as they come. About the only thing I knew for sure was which end of the binoculars to attach to my face. No one offered me a primer on the necessity of burns for maintaining the health of fire-adapted ecosystems. No one told me that the Gila National Forest was smack in the middle of a highly flammable swath of the American Southwest, although I would learn soon enough. At the time I didn't care much about fire. I mostly marveled at the fact that I had stumbled into a paid writing retreat with beaucoup views. I studied the maps and listened closely to the voices on my radio. I wanted to be good enough at the essentials of the job to keep being asked back.

The next season changed my relationship with the country— or rather gave me the beginnings of one. Throughout the summer of 2003, I sat in my tower enthralled as the Dry Lakes Fire meandered through the southern portion of the Gila Wilderness, scarring nearly 100,000 acres in the end. At night spots of open flame glowed on the horizon like bonfires at a reunion of nomadic tribes. By day an observer plane kept in contact with ground crews, monitoring the progress of the burn from above. On my two-way radio, I heard talk of how the fire was "backing slowly off the ridge tops" and "burning nicely in the pondo" and "doing exactly what we want it to." The smoke was beautiful to behold, a vast conglomeration of lazy white gossamer pennants rippling in the wind, and the language used to describe it unfailingly affirmative. The sunsets were bonkers, the mornings redolent of campfire. I was astonished. I was hooked.

Every autumn thereafter, when the fire season was over, I would visit a fresh burn scar somewhere in the forest's 3.3 million acres, poking around in the char. Far from being barren hellscapes devoid of life, as I had imagined, the burn scars quickly became magnets for birds, small mammals, black bears, deer, and elk. It was true that the disturbance to the land left an eerie calm at first, since anything that could run, fly, burrow, or slither away did so, but the initial post-fire rain jump-started a whole series of complex interactions, beginning with the formation of new communities of mosses and fungi in the uppermost layer of soil. Wood-boring insects found new homes in standing snags. Woodpeckers and sapsuckers pecked away at the flourishing insect life. Rodents emerged from their burrows to thrive on the regrowth of seed-bearing forbs and grasses, fattening into targets for hawks and owls. Elk and deer foraged on the leaves of replicating aspen. Bears found sustenance in new little colonies of raspberries and gooseberries, and in acorns from resprouting oak. For some forms of life, of course, wildfire signaled the end of the dance. For others it represented the first notes of a new song.

In 1978 the Gila had announced that, for the first time in any national forest anywhere in the US, an area of 30,000 acres in the Wilderness would be allowed to burn in "prescribed natural fires" if the conditions were right—a belated recognition that the land had burned for millennia, with no paramilitary force in place to stamp out smokes until the first years of the 20th century. At the time it was a radical leap to think of that much of the forest being allowed to burn in one fire.

Thirty-four years later, and a decade into my education in the combustible realities of the Gila, an area ten times that went up in smoke. During the autumn of 2012, I hiked into the southern fringes of the Whitewater-Baldy Fire scar, which I had watched burn for several weeks that May and June from my tower thirty miles away. I had inhaled its downwind smoke, even peered through the scrim of it one evening directly at a solar eclipse, sans protective eyewear—the smokescreen was protection enough. Having spread across nearly 300,000 acres, the fire became by far the biggest in the recorded history of New Mexico. The smoke plume on the day it blew up, when a high-wind event pushed two separate fires together into a roaring monster, resembled nothing I had ever seen in nature, an angry aubergine band smeared across my northern horizon like a brushstroke from the hand of a demented god.

The burn had been cold twelve weeks by the time I had the chance to backpack up Little Dry Creek, then on toward the high peaks of the Gila Wilderness. The landscape seemed to pulse with color under gray, monsoon-season skies. Rain fell each day, and fog swallowed the better part of every afternoon, but the color palette remained vivid. Whorls of red and gold and silver from various minerals in the soil runoff decorated the rich black mud in the creek bottom. Dead needles on standing conifers shone a brilliant orange where trees had succumbed to the heat of ground fire. Torched snags, some on the ground, some still rooted like candlesticks—casualties of a raging crown fire, the flames having jumped straight from treetop to treetop—loomed eerily skeletal through the mist. Here and there eruptions of green poked through the blanket of black: oak sprouts on south-facing slopes, aspen shoots already hip high on north-facing slopes, New Mexico locust scattered amid both. Wildflowers bloomed in manic profusion from big patches of bare soil, impressionistic daubs of yellow, purple, red, and blue. It was all very beautiful—and still I couldn't help but feel the loss.

Our long 20th-century war on fire made big burns such as Whitewater-Baldy so outside the norm they felt like wounds not just to landscapes but also to the human psyche. Partly this was due to the time scale at work. Stand-replacement fires, the kind that burned with high intensity, killing all the living trees across a wide area, had been the rule for the spruce-fir belt in this part of the world. But they tended to happen in any given place just once every hundred years at most, making them outside the course of normal events in a human lifetime—and almost unheard of in the Forest Service era, post-1900. They also tended to be confined to discreet patches of forest, a few hundred or a thousand acres, whereas the Whitewater-Baldy Fire burned at stand-replacing severity over numerous contiguous patches of as much as 5,000 acres apiece.

Even on the Gila, which stood at the vanguard of letting some burns do their thing, we still suppressed more than 90% of all new smokes each year, out of an excess of caution and adherence to institutional habits. We wanted it to burn "on our terms," we sometimes said, so when it came time to let loose some fire on the land, we found it easiest to let the mid-elevation ponderosa savannah succumb to flames. It had always burned more frequently than the spruce-fir higher up the mountains, and the big open areas of grass guaranteed easier ignition, faster spread, and sizeable burns, even as fire intensity rarely got out of hand. In the ponderosa there wasn't enough heavy fuel to let it get out of hand, and containment lines representing the "maximum manageable area" of a burn could be built by improving existing trails across the ridges and mesas well in advance of fire reaching them, and lighting backfires at strategic moments as the main fire approached.

Allowing fires to burn in the high country took much more patience. They could be slow to take hold in the cool, shaded timber that was snowed in half the year, but the bureaucracy did not reward patience when it came to wildfire. Agency protocol demanded that decisions on whether to suppress or let burn be made quickly upon detection, and the easiest thing to do in the high country was to drop a couple of smokejumpers or fly in a helitack crew to fell a few trees and scrape a quick line and call it victory. This foreclosed the risk of a dry spell setting in and combining with a wind event to set the dense spruce and fir to torching with ungodly flame lengths and eruptions of black smoke—the sort of fire prone to light up the switchboard in the supervisor's office with calls from a terrified public.

Playing with fire held risks, of course, but so did suppression. The impulse to fight fires had stunted the evolution of an ever-changing mosaic of areas that were lightly or partially burned in the mixed conifer and spruce-fir. Such a patchwork of forest in sundry phases of recovery from fire, with occasional open meadows and plenty of aspen pockets mingled among the conifers, represented an insurance policy against a megafire. Ask any lookout on the Gila, and she could rattle off a list of fires by name—a dozen or a hundred depending on length of service—that, if allowed to burn, could have helped create the mosiac of forest types that would have prevented Whitewater-Baldy from blowing up as big as it did.

Another way to think about it is that every single fire ever suppressed in the Mogollon Mountains made Whitewater-Baldy a little bit bigger and a little bit hotter than it would have been otherwise. Others have said it before me, and I have elsewhere borrowed their words, but it's worth saying again: we thought we were putting out fires when in fact we were only putting them off.

Later in the autumn of 2012 I visited the burn scar of the McKnight Fire, just northwest of my lookout. For decades it held the record as the state's biggest fire: 50,000 acres of the Black Range high country, ignited by the spontaneous combustion of sawdust at a logging operation in 1951. At the time it was judged an appalling and irreversible catastrophe, and many in the Forest Service hoped that with rapid detection and overwhelming suppression we would never again see its kind. (Rapid detection and the deployment of more than 700 firefighters made little difference to its final size, but no matter.) Six decades later, with its brilliant display of fall color, this scar was a vivid teaching aid in ecological succession, the process by which one forest type replaces another in the aftermath of a major disturbance. Here and there a standing snag rose like an iron spire, a reminder of the forest that was. Aspen and oak in subtly varying shades of yellow painted the top of the range, encircling remnant islands of unburned conifers. Beneath the aspen—the major colonizing species on the high peaks—young conifer reproduction had begun, on its way to taking over again if the country stayed free of fire for another twenty years. In the limpid light of a New Mexico autumn, the whole top of the range appeared to tremble with a magic aura, a technicolor dream coat of saffron and copper and gold.

Most of those lovely leaves and nearly all of the young conifers would burn and run black through feeder streams of the Rio Grande before nine months had passed, in a fire I would spot when it was nothing but a single smoldering tree.

IF YOU HANG AROUND long enough to make it a real vocation, you find that being a conscientious lookout demands a bookkeeper's attention to detail. The popular image of the work leans on its romantic grandeur, its resplendent solitude, but the dirty little secret is that the job deals heavily in numbers. Radio frequencies, personnel call signs, GPS coordinates, fire azimuths, fire legals, fire acreages, lightning-activity levels, Haines indices, maximum wind gusts, the precise details of crew-supply orders, military time to the minute of any noteworthy event, anywhere on your turf: it all goes into a logbook so a question from a dispatcher or a firefighter can be answered at a glance.

There are, of course, many days when nothing of consequence happens, and the log shows little more than a weather report. To take one example from my note-keeping, consider June 6, 2013: the day before the lightning strike that started the Silver Fire. Aside from weather observations, my notes for the day consist of the following:

0700—In service
1900—Out of service

No day hikers, no fires, no traffic on the radio: from an official standpoint, the story of this day is *nada*.

There was, however, another thread to the day, this one contained in a different notebook, unconnected with my duties for the US government, and more evocative of emotional weather than of the atmospheric sort. Most evenings I added to this other notebook at the sturdy wood table in the cabin on my mountain, where by the light of a gas lamp I wrote to keep myself company and make myself real—more of a challenge, some days, than one might think.

That particular evening I wandered the uppermost contours of the peak until the twilight drained over the lip of the western horizon. I began my mosey by visiting a clump of cactus on the mountain's east slope. From there I moved on to a spruce tree on the north face, a mere ninety steps away. The first was indicative of the shrublands life zone, the second of the subalpine, and their proximity—flora typically found two life zones away from each other—reminded me that I inhabited a unique place of overlapping biomes, where desert life forms coexisted with those more typical of the Canadian boreal forest. Slopes with a southern aspect tended to be more open and more arid, while those with a northern exposure harbored more moisture and, as a result, a denser canopy and bigger trees. Since I lived on a mountaintop, I could move from one to the other in the time it took to recite a couple of stanzas of poetry.

From the spruce I continued northwest toward a decadent aspen stand. I circled back to visit a bonsai pine tree anchored in cliff rock on the top of a wind-blasted ridge. Over the years I had come to think of this walk as a stroll through a gallery of loved ones.

Having more than once been called a tree hugger, I had chosen to ignore the derision implicit in the label and instead accept it as a thoughtful suggestion. On this day, as on many others, I moved through the woods making contact with my favorites, most of them living, a few dead but still rooted: the bushy limber pine, the gnarled old Doug fir, the funky aspen with the split trunk. This was their home. I was merely a seasonal resident. It behooved me to pay my respects, say my hellos.

When the veil of dark descended, I built a small outdoor fire and laid on my back next to it, looking up at the stars, recalling all I had seen in the day just past—preparing, in a little while, to make it manifest with words by the light of the lamp in the cabin. *From the mountain you see the mountain*, Ralph Waldo Emerson had written. As spring tilted toward summer that year, I began to believe the gnomic bard had been off by one word.

From the mountain you see *into* the mountain.

Or perhaps it saw into me:

The tenor of a day can be altered by a surprise glimpse of lemon-yellow lichen on ochre rock. This the mountain has taught me; time then for a walk. No sight of turkeys, but arrow-shaped turkey tracks imprinted on the dust of the trail. A family of claret cup cacti in bloom on a hidden prow of cliff: all of them a brilliant red but for one orange outlier, a freak flying a different flag. Bear tracks along a contour of the north-slope meadow, mule deer droppings among the wild iris blooms—mammalian presences perceptible in their leavings. The limbs of a dead tree cradling the trunk of a living leaner, aspen leaves ashimmer in the day's last light. Virga drifting from a few fuzzed clouds. A night hawk beginning the figure-eight flight of its dusk-light hunt. An owl just visible in the gloom, circling. Beyond it the first star-winks in the gathering black. These things have the power to redeem the darkest mood. A privileged glimpse of the old, wild world. Tools with which to pick the lock on the cage of the self. The heart of the mountain beats audibly if you know how to listen. I holler from the cliff's edge. No answer but my echo in the canyon below. Precisely the answer I want.

One could call it an evening like any other in the life of a Wilderness lookout—solitary, sublime, the culmination of yet another day spent dazzled by the sweep of light on desert landforms—yet such notations from a twilight walk, like the official log entries of the workday before them, only ever tell a partial story. For each relic of the urge to render the experience of living alone on a mountain irrevocably in ink—an urge, as I have mentioned, indulged in part to ward off loneliness and forestall disintegration—there is an unseen context, a sort of background music, in this case the dirge of illness and loss.

OVER THE PREVIOUS WINTER my marriage had collapsed. I was left disoriented by the fact that my closest companion for a decade had morphed into an enemy with whom I could no longer speak the simplest words without misunderstanding. I had known men in my position, newly bachelors and surprised by the fact, who consoled themselves with the idea that despite everything they had lost, they had also relieved themselves of their one major pain in the posterior. In an effort to distract myself from sorrow and self-loathing—and from any real reckoning with my failures as a husband—I tried that attitude on for size. The universe having a diabolical sense of humor, it turned out that the pains in my posterior had not even begun.

I decided I needed a change of scenery to match my change in marital status, so I devised a plan to drive to Minnesota and rent a lake cabin close to where I grew up, within reach of all the old ghosts, triggers to the sense memories I hoped to revive as a means of forgetting the present. I loaded up my truck and struck out around eight in the evening, thinking I could make Albuquerque by a little after midnight via back roads. The first 150 miles were uneventful and lovely—a pale moon rising over silhouetted ridge lines dark against a slightly less dark sky. Out north of the little town of Reserve, I encountered a herd of elk crossing the highway. I missed the first one through blind chance. I swerved to miss the second: skill. As with so many things in life, the third time was the charm.

I have seen many brilliant and breathtaking gymnastics moves in my time, but never in person, and none quite like the double somersault with a twist performed by elk number three as it hit the grill of my truck, twirled up onto the hood, bounced off the windshield, and dismounted over the top of the cab. The truck immediately died by the side of the road. The elk took awhile to die in the ditch behind me. I waited two hours for someone to pass by and offer help. In the meantime I listened to the moaning of the elk and the howling of coyotes who surely smelled blood, and regretted all the while not having packed my gun. My truck spent the next six weeks in intensive care in the town of Quemado, at the auto repair shop of the very kind man who towed me there at two in the morning and put me up on his couch.

So much for returning to my roots.

Four months of couch-surfing later, and four weeks before I was scheduled to ascend the mountain for the season that would bring the Silver Fire, I fell ill with a prostate gland so inflamed by infection it felt like an angry blowfish at the center of my being: the perfect manifestation of a deep soul sickness. The pain, combined with fever, gave me nights of agony near enough to unbearable that I found myself looking longingly at my shotgun as a potential source of permanent relief. I lost thirty pounds in thirty days; I couldn't tolerate the thought of seeing visitors, much less them seeing me. This was not what I had in mind when I imagined my resumption of bachelor living: wandering fruitlessly from urologist to urologist, fearful my erotic life was but a memory.

One close friend offered to supply me with groceries, and for a month she was the only person I allowed through the door, although not very often, since my appetite had vanished. I quit leaving the house, didn't bother answering the phone. What was there to say? The first course of antibiotics had caused achilles tendon pain so severe it rendered me unable to walk for two weeks, a not unknown side effect of Ciprofloxacin. The second course of antibiotics had caused a severe allergic reaction after just one dose, a not unknown side effect of Bactrim. The ones prescribed in place of them had failed to have any effect, a not uncommon outcome of throwing Doxycycline like a Hail Mary pass at a prostate infection.

Having run the gamut on the pharmaceutical options for treating my condition, I was told by the doctors it was now chronic and likely permanent. They had done all they could to help. They wrote me off and wished me luck.

John called a couple of times after he heard I was sick, but I didn't bother calling back. All of a sudden, at the age of forty, I had become a man I no longer recognized, and at the same time a bit of a cliché—bound up in a dubious mortgage, tangled in impersonal legal proceedings with a soon-to-be ex-wife, and ravaged by untreatable pain in my most sensitive bodily organs—a middle-aged loser in the casino of American life, in other words. I didn't want to talk about any of it, and John was the last guy in the world you wanted checking in with you if you didn't want to talk about something.

I had been avoiding his calls for months by then. He began trying to reach me when he found out I had left my wife. Each time his voice appeared on my answering machine, every two or three weeks, I deleted it without listening to the end of the message. I could not bear the thought of going over the story of the split in the kind of detail he typically demanded. Living through it had been lurid enough, and recounting the story in its totality, I feared, would reproduce the confusion and pain, a pain I wanted more than anything to forget. I knew John would not let me forget. I knew he believed with an almost religious fervor that only by confronting that which caused us pain could we avoid becoming its prisoner. So I ignored him, chose instead to romance my bitter solitude, and thus remained unaware he was going through a similar breakup with his girlfriend Lee, who had shown him love was still possible after the loss of Miquette. My self-absorption blinded me to the fact that he was calling in part because he needed me, not merely because he thought I needed him.

One day he came knocking unannounced. By then I hadn't seen him in half a year. He betrayed no disappointment in me, no hard feelings. He held a container of chicken paprika in one hand and two cigarettes in the other, a sparkle-eyed grin on his face even as he winced at the sight of me. "One of them's good for you," he said, looking down at the gifts in his hands, "but I'm not sure which. Maybe we should try both." I smiled in spite of myself, a peculiar contortion of my face I hadn't felt in longer than I cared to remember.

We took his food to the back patio, where we ate from bowls while standing, a courtesy he did me because he knew I couldn't sit.

He told me he had been thinking a lot about a problem of the lookout's life: how maybe once a decade a fire pops up on your turf just when you've gone to the outhouse or left the tower to stretch your legs or do a little project work on the ground, radio in hand, as always. Sometimes, just in that moment, another lookout sees the smoke and calls over the radio, seeking a cross of azimuths. John wanted to devise some sort of code we could use to cover for ourselves if we weren't in the tower. The code he proposed was for the one caught unawares to reply, "You know, I was just looking over there, thinking I might have seen something. Let me get the binoculars and have another peek"—then boogie up the tower to get the coordinates.

This was clever, no doubt about it, just the sort of cheekiness that made John so dear. It was also a means of hiding ignorance beneath the cloak of premonition to everyone else listening on that radio frequency, essentially all of our colleagues. But I was pretty sure I would have no need for any secret code, not that summer: the five miles on foot to my mountain were way beyond my powers just then, and I felt the possibility of my twelfth summer there slipping away. John refused to offer false encouragement. He simply persisted with his bid to bring me into his friendly conspiracy, which was, in its way, a form of encouragement.

"The only question is which of us will be caught with our pants down first and need to use the code," he said. "Whoever it is, that guy buys dinner for the other."

When I looked back on the time of my illness, I saw that I never again felt quite as bad as I did the moment before John showed up at my door with dinner and a postprandial smoke. Perhaps it was merely coincidence. I'm not ascribing him magical healing powers. The remedy for my ailment remained months away, the food he had prepared was mediocre, the cigarette tasted awful. Each of us was merely a social smoker, on "special occasions," and as John pointed out, what could possibly be more special, hard on the heels of a marital implosion, than a belated fortieth-birthday present of a prostate like a spiny blowfish? Delivered in a voice both sly and sensitive, this situational assessment was exactly the sort that could make a man forget to feel terrible about himself for a moment, by holding up a mirror to the absurdity and even the bleak comedy of his condition. Maybe that was the thing I needed right then: an ability to finally laugh at myself, at just how pathetically my life had gone off the rails.

MY RECOVERY, AS MENTIONED, took some time in arriving—and took a profound leap of faith of the sort perhaps only a desperate man could make. That leap of faith involved availing myself of the tender ministrations of a woman I nicknamed, with all due affection, Lady Magic Finger, the details of whose healing modalities John found engrossing when I eventually mustered the courage to share them with him just weeks before his death.

He was delighted to learn the backstory. It began when an overseas radio network called me in 2011 to request an interview with a living fire lookout *in situ*. Fire season on the Gila had just ended, but I arranged to drive up John's mountain and have a conversation by phone, while standing on the catwalk of his tower. The network wanted high-quality audio of my end of the conversation, so it hired a radio reporter on a freelance gig to record me with a mic while I talked on her cell. Mónica was the reporter they found for the job.

Although she had lived most of her life a three-hour drive away, she had never been to the Gila. The view from Signal Peak amazed her, this piece of wild country, so close to home, that had the look of nothing she had ever seen. Afterward, eager to learn more about the place, she began poking around, searching for stories to report. It didn't take long for the country to oblige, beginning with the biggest fire in state history, nine months after we met. I became a background source for that story, and a link to others who knew more than me. In this way our friendship was born, and platonic friendship it remained for two years.

When my marriage collapsed, though, I sensed a change in the emotional weather between us.

The mutual respect demonstrated by our friendship convinced her that perhaps we were destined for more. Despite every impulse to the contrary—newly single and decidedly skittish about romantic enganglements, not to mention the signals being sent from Prosty the Blowfish—I agreed to her overture to take me out for my birthday the autumn after the Silver Fire, dinner and drinks in downtown Ciudad Juárez, ten minutes from her home in El Paso. I had always enjoyed her company and admired her mind. I figured our outing would at least offer me the chance to explain, face to face, how unworthy of her attention I was, how broken a man.

It was no lie, no pantomime of modesty. After sitting for three hours in my truck to get there, I found that sitting through dinner tipped me into pain beyond description amid polite company. I had a fire inside of me that would not go out, and whatever it was she thought she saw when she looked at me, I assured her she was mistaken. She could do better.

She asked if there was any way she could help. I told her I didn't think so. All that was left for me to try was an ancient remedy I had come across in my research, a practice called milking the prostate—or, more prosaically, prostate massage—which was the subject of more than a few good jokes but had gone out of favor with the advent of potent antibiotics that, as my case proved, still sometimes failed. I couldn't imagine anyone I knew performing such a procedure. The very thought of it gave new meaning to that old familiar phrase from my Catholic youth, "the mortification of the flesh."

To my surprise she immediately offered to give it a try.

"What is there to lose?" she asked.

"My dignity, for one thing."

"Don't be silly," she said. "The thing to try to lose is the pain. Lose that, and your dignity will take care of itself."

I had experienced my share of first dates over the years, some of which had ended awkwardly, but this was something else.

Having begun our romance with such a radical act of trust, we could hardly do otherwise than proceed in that fashion thereafter.

When I told this story to John, the only friend to whom I could imagine admitting something so intimate, so bizarre, we shared a ribald round of laughter at the fact that my ability to take any enjoyment from life—to sit for a meal or a movie, to drive, to make love—hinged on my submitting to a program of what he called "therapeutic ass play," conducted with the aid of water-based lubricant and powder-free, beaded-cuff, non-latex rubber gloves. The whole ordeal had the shape of a parable about the quasi-religious faith with which we ingest the fruits of corporate chemistry to treat problems better solved by human touch. I had gobbled pills when what I needed was a laying on of hands. The pills had done nothing to help, had in fact done me nothing but harm. Only a firm and well-placed finger saved me, and John did not surprise me when he spun this as a blessing in disguise.

"Every guy on the planet should have the experience of being penetrated by a woman," he said. "Especially us poor bastards who grew up Catholic, fearing nothing more than rear entry from a foreign object. I think it would make us all better men. So congrats on becoming a better man. You didn't even have to try very hard. Just drop your drawers and presto bingo."

Afterward, each time I heard behind me the satisfying snap on Mónica's wrist from those beaded-cuff, powder-free, non-latex rubber gloves, I thought to myself: I am about to be a better man.

It was true in more ways than one.

But like the fire that would change my mountain forever, that was all still in the unseen country of the future on that evening when John assured me I would soon be back on the lookout—and in this too he was right. One month after his surprise visit with the chicken paprika, still weak and wobbly from too long spent in bed, barely able to sit long enough to drive myself the hour to the trailhead, and somewhat of a suppurating wound emotionally speaking—not yet on the path to becoming a better man—I nonetheless stood on my elevated patch of *querencia,* later than planned but not too late, alone in the place where I felt most myself in the world. As I stared down the fact of my fragility that spring, I ached not only with a pain in my privates but with a desire to re-embrace the wild beauty of the mountain, to touch its ancient energies, see deeper into its mysteries—no doubt as a means of transcending that pain. Appropriate, perhaps, that around that time I would add to my commonplace book a passage from Chuck Bowden: *I try to read nature books but I do not know what they are talking about. There is no booze, women seem to be shunned, the men also do not appear on the pages. There is this quality of a life without a heartbeat, loins without juice, breasts without nipples, britches without a bulge.*

Also, it went without saying, no inflamed sex glands, please. My malady not only didn't belong in a nature book, it hardly appeared in serious literature at all, aside from afflicting Steinbeck's dog in *Travels with Charley.* In my rather desperate search for anything of enduring value ever written on the subject of my condition, I found precisely one book, by the novelist, critic, and fellow sufferer Tim Parks, in which I underlined a single passage, a quote from a pamphlet handed him by a young urologist: *It has to be born in mind that the chances of a complete recovery from prostatitis are minimal, almost nonexistent in fact. Prostatitis sufferers tend to be restless, worrisome, dissatisfied individuals who drag their miseries around from one doctor to the next in search of a cure they never find. The urologist must be careful not to let himself be demoralized by these people and their intractable pathologies.* To which Parks appended: *The urologist must be careful! Poor fellow.*

While expressing sympathy for the doctor over the patient, the pamphlet alluded to a phenomenon common to sufferers of chronic prostatitis—an emotional state called "catastrophizing." I knew it well. The pain becomes so debilitating, and goes on for so long, that the mind can no longer see a way out. The future appears a total ruin. One begins to feel as if only a miracle can stave off catastrophe, and miracles, as we know, are in short supply.

Nonetheless, I had come to the mountain that summer secretly hoping for a profound intervention from an unseen source. I would get exactly what I wished for, just not in the form I had imagined.

Now, when I look back on my notebook entry from the night before the big fire, I conjure the final twilight of a vanished world, a high mountain forest poised on the pivot of before and after, an owl in the gloaming like an omen. And I hear an echo of Joan Didion:

Keepers of private notebooks are a different breed altogether, lonely and resistant rearrangers of things, anxious malcontents, children afflicted apparently at birth with some presentiment of loss.

BEING CONSCRIPTED for public relations work and light clerical duty in a government office was John's and my shared nightmare, and the summer of the Silver Fire the nightmare came true for me. With the lookout closed in the wake of my evacuation, my boss Dennis couldn't think of a way to make use of me in the woods, so he handed me over to colleagues who turned me into an all-purpose gofer of the sort that answers telephones and inventories office supplies. Five days of that put me thirty-nine hours beyond my tolerance for flourescent lighting in any given week, and by the end of it I was close to being a candidate for long sleeves and padded walls. As fortune would have it, my stint as an office monkey lined up with Jean's days off her tower. She stopped by the office one afternoon in order to turn in her time sheet, just as I was making photocopies of campground-closure notices. She took one look at me and said, "You do not seem happy."

A fellow Midwesterner like me and John, Jean was keenly attuned to the mental weather of people she cared about. She was also a skilled diplomat with a nose for logistics, always willing to coax and cajole the chain of command in order to make things happen. All of her most subtle talents in that realm were required to negotiate a deal that sprang me from my workday prison.

It just so happened that around that time another mountain on the forest lost its primary lookout due to medical emergency. A firefighter stepped in to cover the open shifts, but that was merely a stopgap. Jean devised an elegant plan whereby her relief lookout, Jim Cox, agreed to cover for our sick colleague. I would cover for Jim, and Jean would give up a couple of her regularly scheduled work days to grant us both alternating eight-day runs. It was the same schedule as the one worked by Sara and Ráz, with an overlap day every Wednesday as one of them hiked into the mountain, the other out. This thoughtful and selfless move on Jean's part kept me employed at what I do best—looking out the window—and, as an added benefit, made for a decent vantage on the Silver Fire.

Jean's mountain offered not only a different view but a different experience than I was accustomed to. The lookout there lived in the tower, a twelve-by-twelve-foot room. Cooking, eating, sleeping, and standing watch all took place in the same 144 square feet of real estate. Over the years I had come to appreciate the fact that my tower was no more than a spartan office, seven-by-seven, and that my domestic duties and my work duties played out in separate realms. Despite the roomier tower, the merging of living space and office space made me feel slightly claustrophobic. I compensated by bathing more frequently than I would have on my peak. On days of clear skies—most days that June—I used showering as an excuse to get out of the tower for a while in the afternoon. Water was plentiful in the cistern, and Jean's three-gallon shower bag heated quickly with the sun burning overhead. I hung it from the roof of the supply cabin below the tower, confident I would not be interrupted by a random visitor. During the twenty-four discontinuous days I spent there, I saw one hiker.

With smoke billowing in the distance by day and the top of the Black Range glowing orange and crimson by night, I wandered in my mind over the particulars of that high mountain forest as I had known them, places I had come to love more than any others on Earth. Most days I spent an hour or two working on a crude map of things that may not have existed any longer. There was no way to be sure. I revisited in memory the ruins of an old line cabin on a hidden bench just below the crest trail. I recalled an aspen tree with a dendroglyph from 1922 carved in its bark, and I remembered a series of old Douglas firs with ceramic insulators wired high on their trunks, relics of the telephone line that once ran from the lookout to the guard station in the foothills. All of them human artifacts, I realized: just the sorts of things a wildfire in a Wilderness would devour, maybe even should devour, as a reminder of our human transience.

On one hot and windy day in late June, the fire chewed through 10,000 acres and blew up into a smoke plume that rose to the top of the troposphere. It was capped by a pyrocumulus cloud from which could be heard the rumble of thunder, the fire having created its own weather. The main column of heat resembled a shimmering sword of smoke piercing the cloud above it—easily one of the most astounding sights I had ever witnessed, as hot air exploded upward and cool air rushed into the burn from all sides, feeding the fire with fresh oxygen. According to John, charred oak leaves fluttered to the ground like wounded birds below the tower on Signal Peak, more than twenty miles away as the crow flew.

Absorbed as I was in my smoke-plume gawking, I sometimes forgot I was living inside another fire scar, the Bull Fire of seven years earlier. It had roamed the land for weeks in 2006 and singed nearly 80,000 acres—a mostly calm, low-intensity burn, allowed to do its thing. Jean had lived with smokejumpers on the mountain for a week and a half as they cleared brush and created a fire break to protect her tower, waiting all the while for the flames to arrive. Their bivouack site, which they christened "Camp Patience"— complete with thronelike seats carved from a big ponderosa trunk and arranged around a stone fire circle—remained intact out toward the mountain's helispot. Evidence of the burn itself was still visible in every direction, although the blackened bark on the dead and living trees was muted by the vibrant leaves of healthy young oak and the waxy green needles of ponderosa saplings.

When the rains set in that July, I made a circuit of the mountain every evening, as I would have on my own peak, angling first along the north-facing ridge below the tower, dining on gooseberries from the bushes sprouting there. Plucked with care—ideally by the withered brown bud at the bottom of the fruit—and split open between my front teeth, they spilled their sweet flesh and didn't hurt the tongue despite their armor of spines. Their existence was a direct result of the Bull Fire. I had it to thank for my nightly dessert.

Meanwhile, I kept up my habit of writing down the days:

It's Independence Day and I'm socked in by rain. The temperature dropped so suddenly I lit a fire in the wood stove to stay warm.

Yesterday I witnessed the best lightning storm I've seen in years. It rolled in after dark and strobed the sky with capillaries of light, cloud-to-cloud strikes with weird fringes and jagged arcs, and ground hits that along with the wind made the tower rock and roll. Earlier in the day I spotted a smoke in Chicken Coop Canyon, a single snag struck by lightning: a crew flew in on a helicopter and quashed it. Even the Silver Fire has been reduced by rain to not much more than a minor smudge of smoke in Black Canyon. No more plumes or open flames. It's in the books. The season has turned.

It's cozy in the tower with the wood stove cooking. Lightning stabs to the north; heavy rain falls to the west and southwest. Two pink smears of cloud hang above Eagle Peak. The forest has a cool, blue-black look to it, and the Gambel's oak thickets shiver in the breeze. Low rumbles echo in the canyons and shake the ridge tops. I sit in the tower sipping tea. Nothing to do but plenty to see.

It's still a little odd to be here. I'm too accustomed to a certain view, certain trails, a certain setup for cooking and using water—everything here is different. I respect Jean's space and am trying to leave everything as untouched by my presence as possible. (My frequent bathing, I tell myself, is as much for her as for me: I remember what she once said about her hypersensitive nose, and I recall stinky Barry, the relief lookout whose body odor lingered in the tower for hours after our shift transitions.) I'm as much a creature of habit as she is. She runs a damn tight ship—she has to, living and working in a twelve-by-twelve room—and I only want to leave the place ever so slightly better than I found it when she shared it with me. Just as she's done all these years here. Just as I've done on my peak.

Even though it sits on public land, open to all who can walk or ride a horse, I sometimes think of my mountain as my own personal kingdom. Unaccountable arrogance, no doubt—I'm merely

1/300-millionth part-owner like any American—but it is true that I'm the one who gets to live there a hundred days a year, and it's not as if I run off visitors by brandishing a gun. The mountain doesn't belong to me. I belong to the mountain. I'm nagged by a sense of nostalgia for the way it was and I'm anxious to see what's changed, what burned and what was spared. What does the place look like now? Not knowing is a kind of torture. To have been airlifted out, as good a story as that makes for winter bull sessions at the Buffalo Bar, still stings a little bit—to have been denied an ongoing, front-row seat for the big one. Then again, it's not as if I didn't have fair warning. Quite the contrary. Two years ago I saw the Wallow Fire, 538,000 acres, largest in Arizona history, just across the state line from the Gila (in fact a little finger crossed the border near Luna), its smoke blotting out my western horizon, its origin sixty miles from my tower on a straight line. Then last year gave us the Whitewater-Baldy Fire, largest in New Mexico history, 297,000 acres and only half as far from my mountain as the Wallow. I remember the taste of it, the smell. There was no good reason to think my neighborhood wouldn't be next.

I wonder why I'm so nostalgic and sentimental for places. Maybe it has something to do with growing up on a farm we lost to the bankers. So many times over the years I've returned there in search of something from my past I cannot name, and every time I discover that the place is more real in my imagination than it is when I stand upon it. The buildings are gone, the grove of trees is gone: all of it burned to the ground in a training exercise by the local VFD. In order for it not to vanish entirely, I've had to keep it alive in my memory. Maybe that established a pattern for all the places I've loved since. Perhaps it even accounts for my attraction to burn scars—the fact that my original home on Earth was erased in flames. Conversations, even the names of people, often just drift away from me unless I write them down while they're still fresh, but I can remember the rooms where I lived fifteen years ago in Missoula, Montana, as if I stepped away from them yesterday. None of the places I've loved have been spared transformation. Houses, apartments, neighborhoods, landscapes— every single place I've ever lived has changed in significant ways, and often I feel the change as a kind of desecration.

Maybe that's simply a result of growing older and imagining a time and place of lost innocence. Or maybe it's just the price of living in a society as restless and dynamic and omnivorous as ours, a society that has little use for that which does not generate profit, and everywhere discards and dishonors the past. Southern Minnesota has mostly been cleansed of its small farmers and wildlife. Missoula is deep into the process of being Californicated. The island of Manhattan has become an urban theme park, one giant upscale mall for the rich and shameless.

I should know by now that nothing lasts and nothing stays the same. My life has been one long lesson in that fact. I want, I suppose, one place I can hold to as immutable, one thing I can count on as fixed. But of course I already have that: the guarantee that I won't be here forever. The knowledge that transformation awaits me too, the transition to nonbeing. I am as ephemeral as the details of any place. More so, given that once I'm gone, the places will remain. So I scribble to mark my passage through those places I have loved most.

WHEN ITS GROWTH CEASED, four weeks after it began, the Silver Fire had moved across 138,705 acres, or 214 square miles. It lived on through the rains for an additional week or two in scattered stump holes, burning in the roots of trees it had already consumed aboveground, sending up smoke signals from the underside of the Earth.

Dennis granted me permission to return to my mountain in the final week of July. "Don't get too depressed up there," he said. "Remember, a big fire is just the birthday for the next forest. It will be green again before long."

It was a peculiar hike in, that first time back. Much of the walk was lacking in living vegetation. It made me feel a little vulnerable to move through the landscape, visible as I was from a distance. Then I remembered the burn area was still under a closure order: the country was entirely mine, for a little while anyway. No one would see me but the birds. Still, it felt spooky to be so exposed in a place where the forest had once provided the shade of an intermittent canopy. Now there was no proper canopy, just a bare etching of black branches against a pale blue sky. On a trail I had hiked so often I could make my way along it in the dark, I felt as if I were having the inverse of a déjà vu experience—traveling through a familiar place made newly strange.

The view to the south, where the fire first got up and ran, encompassed a stunning tableau of destruction, a 10,000-acre patch of forest transformed into charcoal: a century of accumulated biomass reduced to blackened stalks overnight. It had the naked look of country whose soil structure might unravel with one hard rain. *Yea, though I walk through the valley of the shadow of death,* I thought, as my fireproof Nomex pants accumulated streaks and smudges from burnt branches and fallen logs. I was slowly taking on the camouflage offered by the country—becoming, step by step, one with the char.

Three-quarters of the way to the top, big stands of intact

forest appeared where the fire didn't climb into the crowns of the trees, thanks to a mid-June rain that moderated fire behavior for a weekend. That pause helped preserve my immediate environs far better than I had dared hope, in part by allowing a window of opportunity for a burnout operation. With the smoke and flames tamped down by higher humidity, a helicopter was able to maneuver in close enough to drop ping-pong balls juiced with potassium permanganate and glycol in a big circle around the lookout. When the balls hit the ground they ignited the surface fine fuels but spared the trees above, robbing the Silver Fire of continuous fuel—fire fought with fire. Standing in the middle of the open meadow on the mountain, rejoicing in the sight of the cabin and tower standing unscathed, I could hardly tell there had been a burn in the neighborhood at all. The peak still wore its cap of pine and fir, and the meadow grasses were luxuriant from the rains.

As I made my initial survey of the facilities, something caught my eye in the grass, something bright green and gently quivering. I bent close and studied it: a mountain tree frog. I had heard its telltale croak on occasion, late in previous seasons, usually around the pond on the flank of the mountain, but I had never seen one up on top. I sat down near it, as unthreateningly as possible, and tried to remain as still as it did for the next half hour, my compatriot on an island of green, each of us breathing but otherwise motionless.

It thrilled me as much as any wildlife encounter I had ever experienced, probably because it contrasted so starkly with my pessimistic assumptions of what I would find on my return. Despite a decade of visiting the aftermath of big burns, seeing how quickly the regrowth came, I had arrived expecting only the funereal this time, probably because the changes hit extra close to home. My attachment to the landscape surrounding that mountain had arisen from an ongoing intimacy with all its moods and weathers and creatures. It had been cemented by a fondness for certain special places I had come to think of as sacred, places whose beauty had offered me a lifeline through more than one kind of loss: in the beginning, the death of a brother; more recently, the end of a marriage. With the forest reshaped, I had feared another in a suite of losses whose accumulated weight I struggled to bear.

Many of us who lived in and cared about the American West felt that sense of mounting loss, felt it in our physical beings—our reason for living here rooted in the physical, after all, both the land's and our own. We liked the look and feel and smell of the mountains and we liked to test ourselves in them, hiking, skiing, rock climbing, horseback riding, fly fishing, elk hunting—you name it, there was something for everyone, and big chunks of public land on which to do it. But landscapes we loved were being transformed on a scale that was hard to absorb; entire mountain ranges were burning up. For a hundred years we mostly kept the scorch at bay. We became expert at deploying shock troops in the war on fire, bringing the hurt to an elemental force we convinced ourselves was unnatural. As a result we cultivated a public belief in the idea that our forests were meant to remain forever dense and green, timeless and static. Just as we awoke to the rude fact of our mistake, the fires became bigger and more intense than any we had ever seen, even in places like the Gila, with a decades-long history of aggressive burning, though not quite aggressive enough.

Scorched earth was now the ground we inhabited if we lived in or near the forests of the American West. We often wondered how long it would take for them to "recover" from being burned. Too infrequently did we recall that a charred forest was itself in recovery from having been kept artificially green, by a war fought in our name, and paid for by our tax dollars—a war it seemed would never end, although the battles were often rearguard actions now.

In "Lifetimes With Fire," Gary Snyder wrote: *In 1952 and '53 I worked on fire lookouts in the Skagit District of the Mount Baker forest, northern Washington Cascades. Crater Mountain first and then Sourdough. Those were the first jobs I'd held that I felt had some virtue. Guarding against forest fires, finally I had found Right Occupation. I congratulated myself as I stood up there above the clouds memorizing various peaks and watersheds, for finding a job that didn't contribute to the Cold War and the wasteful modern economy. The joke's on me as I learn fifty years later how much the fire suppression ideology was wrong-headed and how much it has contributed to our current problems.*

I knew that feeling of self-congratulation. I had once bailed on a career in corporate journalism because I came to detest its narrow range of acceptable opinion and its attitude of deference to officially constituted power. With a few vivid exceptions, it mostly served to normalize sociopathic greed and endless war. I wanted no part in buttressing either. Instead I ran away to a lookout tower in the world's first Wilderness and even managed by sheer happenstance to land in a place with an enlightened attitude about fire. I bathed in my sense of good fortune and felt a little smug every time I thought of my friends toiling away at their computers back east, feeding the bottomless maws of the content machines. But the joke was on me as I learned our enlightenment had come too late to prevent huge, abnormally destructive burns in the age of rapid planetary heating. I had arrived seeking freedom and found more than my fair share, the nearest thing on Earth to my own private utopia. True wild in the 21st century was a rare vintage indeed, but I had tasted it. The price was my attendance at what came to feel like a wake for the Holocene.

The miracle of concealed combustion—of the sort found in jet engines and coal-fired power plants, the sort upon which our entire way of life was built—once did us the favor of drawing a discreet curtain between our appetites and the immense heat that made their satisfaction possible, from morning commute to bedtime calibration of the thermostat. The effects of our ongoing resurrection of the Carboniferous, everywhere visible—vanishing glaciers, megafires—no longer granted us any such courtesy. Having exhumed oil and coal from the bowels of the Earth and torched them in world-altering quantities, we now inhabited the space between their origin underground and their destination in the atmosphere: the surface of a planet on fire. From the taiga along the Arctic Circle to the brushlands of Australia, the world was burning up. It wasn't merely my vocation that made me think this a fact best appreciated from a high place, the higher the better. NASA satellites, for instance, showed smoke from the Whitewater-Baldy Fire visible from space in May of 2012. The plume blew several hundred miles across the borders of six states, as far north as Iowa.

In the southern Black Range, the old, green forest lived only in remnants and memories, and some of the memories were mine.

It was a sobering thought, the idea that my mind, if I lived another forty years, might become one of the last repositories on Earth of how certain stands of old growth looked and felt and smelled in a place once called "the wildest Wilderness in the West." At first I wondered whether the fire would deform my connection with the country—whether it would inflict a wound that would forever disfigure my passion for it. Instead I found I loved it more than ever, indeed felt an obligation to continue my annual mountain-sitting retreat for as long as I felt physically able, years into the future I dared hope, in order to see what the place would become, what capability for resilience it possessed, if only we could leave it the hell alone and let it burn.

Ecologists would find plenty to keep them busy in the years to come, cataloging transformations, tallying losses and gains, but any sentient human with an interest in actual science could intuit that more would be lost than gained. As the planet went on heating, the spruce-fir and mixed-conifer forests of the Southwest would continue torching off, destined to pass into legend and lore. Perhaps the amphibians that called them home would one day vanish too: a mountain tree frog at 10,000 feet in the Black Range had nowhere higher—and therefore nowhere cooler—to move to escape warming temperatures. This plot of ground was its final refuge, unless it found a way to hitch a ride on clouds.

It would fall to the poets among us to work up a lament for the unmaking and remaking of our forests, a lament that at the very least accommodated, perhaps even found ways to celebrate, the taste of ash and the color black.

THE NAVEL OF THE WORLD

ANOTHER SUMMER, another burned mountain: it was getting to be a habit. For reasons having to do with both my fear of death and the allure of it—the big dark, the long sleep—I needed to spend some time in the place where John had breathed his last breath. Staring at the Signal Fire scar day after day from John's tower, a fire that never should have happened but which now dominated the view, not to mention the emotional life of the town I called home, with its connection to five deaths in fifteen days—Dr. Hochla, Ella, Michael, Ella Jaz, and John—I came to feel I'd be shirking a duty to bear witness if I didn't venture into the burn. One evening, after going out of service on the radio, I decided it was time for a walk through the ashes.

It didn't take long to discover the scene. The smell tipped me off from fifty yards away. The body of Sundance still lay where he fell, and his bay-colored hide stood out in a landscape that was otherwise monochrome. The bare earth and fire-scarred trees created a black canvas that was now streaked and daubed with white vulture droppings, like a halfway finished Pollock painting. Search-and-rescue volunteers had retrieved John's body, but rules and regs did not call for the removal of a half-ton of horse flesh from national forest land, and the birds had made of the carcass a feast. In the afternoons I sometimes watched them circling the ridge southeast of the tower, as many as two dozen at a time riding thermals over the crest of the divide, spinning in languid gyres, dark against the light blue sky. Lazy-looking but never not vigilant, they reminded me of lookouts with wings.

The trail followed the contour of a steep slope just inside the edge of the burn. Sundance had fallen hard to the downhill side, his neck bent around a charred tree trunk, his shoes still glittering amid the ash. In the two weeks since his fall, his hide had shrunk until it draped over his bones like a tattered blanket. Beneath that blanket, inside the rib cage, something scratched and scrabbled, something alive. I stood and listened for awhile, touched in some very old way—even sort of honored to eavesdrop on the process of flesh reentering the food chain by the traditional method. The sound said all you needed to know about the pickin's being slim: a dry scraping, a sound signifying the carcass had been worked over pretty well already. I tossed a small rock at it, then another, irrationally fearing the appearance of a tiny bear cub, which would imply the presence of Mama nearby.

Instead a vulture's head poked from the body cavity. The bird ducked out into the light, glanced over its shoulder at me, beat its heavy wings, and took flight through the bare branches of the ghost forest: meal interrupted.

The turkey vulture, a study in paradox: from a distance so graceful, gliding on invisible currents, air riffling its fingerlike wing tips; at close range another story, misfortune its sustenance, death what's for dinner. *Your ass is somebody else's meal,* Gary Snyder wrote, in an essay called "The Etiquette of Freedom," and more than once over the years, while thinking of those words, I had imagined my corpse—after an accidental fall from my fire tower—picked clean by *Cathartes aura*, ensuring my remnants would soar one last time over mountains before drifting back to earth as scavenger's excrement. What can I say? The days are long in a lookout tower. A man has to think about something. But not until that moment, as I stood over a fleshless cadaver once called Sundance, had I known by name a creature who had passed through a vulture's digestive system. The old boy had rejoined the chain of life at a new link, and as a devotee of the glorious messiness of the human and the animal, I found myself pleased by the thought.

It occurred to me to wonder whether John might have chosen the same fate, had he been given the option of how to dispose of his corpse ahead of time. It would have been just like him to want to skip the expense of cremation.

IN THE FIRST DAYS AND WEEKS of John's absence, the things I missed most were not his hugs, which were truly unrestrained for a dude from the Upper Midwest, nor his stories, which ran along forever in accumulating details and comic digressions as he teased you toward the climax or the punch line, nor even his invitations to go for a joy ride in his GT40, the car designed by Ford specifically to beat Ferrari at Le Mans in the late 1960s. He would push it to 130 miles per hour on lonely blacktop straightaways, the engine roaring so loudly behind our heads we had to wear earplugs and communicate with hand gestures as the scenery scrolled past in a blur.

All of these things I would attempt to keep in memory, turn to and caress when necessary.

No, what I missed above all was his voice on the two-way radio, a voice inflected with the playful rhythms of the large-hearted trickster he was in person. I suppose I missed it because it was the major way I experienced him during the summers we spent on our respective mountains, his almost due west of mine, a subtle but reassuring hump on the horizon, azimuth 265° and 16' according to the ring around my Osborne Fire Finder. His peak was the first landmark on which I focused to calibrate the sighting device at the beginning of each new season. My instrument wasn't true until I placed myself in perfect relation to him. In his absence I felt my bearings go a little squinky.

A peculiar thing happens once you've been a lookout for many seasons. Radio protocol demands that you forego your given name, identify yourself by the name of your peak, and answer to that name when called, so for several months each year you are not Sara Irving or Rázik Majean, Teresa Beall or Mark Hedge, Jean Stelzer or John Kavchar—you are the name of a mountain. The longer you keep the job, the more your identity becomes entwined with that mountain.

By living and working where we do, we become intimate with the moods of a wild and moody place, its flora and fauna, its susceptibility to extreme weather. We discover which of the north-face snowbanks melts last, where water collects in the rainy season, which trees lure ladybugs by the thousands until their bark turns a writhing orange like some strange, rippling skin. We learn the songs of birds and the names of flowers, the spooky thrill of monsoon-season mornings waking up inside the clouds. We discover where to find food in the time of ripeness— wild raspberries, prickly gooseberries—and where other creatures find theirs. We walk in the footsteps of bears.

We can't help becoming amateur phenologists, noting when the aphids hatch, when the irises bloom, when the Clark's nutcrackers and broadtailed hummingbirds arrive. Scattered across the sky-island ridges in communal vigilance, a club of splendid misfits delightfully at odds with the drift of the culture, we come to feel ourselves a part of something noble, singular, gorgeous, and doomed. Eventually the voices of our fellow lookouts become aural talismans, sources of comfort and connection amid a sometimes enigmatic solitude.

Our terse radio commo ratifies an evolving reality. The work has made of the mountains a gift, and we honor this gift by assuming and intoning their names. John had been Signal Peak, and for every summer of the new millennium Signal Peak had been John, just as Sara and Ráz had merged with their mountain, and Hedge his, and Jean hers. I had accepted reassignment from my own mountain out of respect for John, but no matter how many times I said those two little words, I could not make them comfortable in my mouth, calling in service each morning, calling in my smoke and weather reports. I was not Signal Peak and never would be. Only John could eyeball the sky and, with whimsical precision, call in a morning report of seventeen-and-a-quarter percent cloud cover. Only John would think to name a harmless end-of-season smoke the Jell-O Fire. To have tried such a trick would have marked me as the crassest pretender.

That's not to say I didn't admire things about the place. It was a mountain, after all, 9,000 feet above sea level, and it's hard to be disappointed by a mountain, especially in this part of the world, especially one with a fire tower on top. The view to the northwest ran over wild and crumpled country—encompassing the deep canyon of the Gila River and the aptly named Diablo Range—to a horizon marked by the highest mountains in the region, the Mogollons, just shy of 11,000 feet. To the south the vistas spread a hundred miles most days, deep into the bootheel of New Mexico, where the ramparts of the Animas Mountains and the Big Hatchets could be seen through an aqueous scrim of desert heat. They weren't the sort of peaks that would have caught the eye of Ansel Adams, but they did have an aura of isolated majesty about them, rising from the tilted plain like phantasmagorical pyramids. Their presence on the horizon almost forgave the defining feature of the middle distance in that direction: the gleaming rooftop of the Walmart superstore in Silver City.

Almost.

A visitor had once called the tower a "honey-colored box in the sky," due to the lustrous finish on the pine cabinets John had installed. The tower was thirty feet tall, erected in 1932, with a cab updated in the 1960s, fourteen feet square, encircled by a catwalk: altogether more spacious and comfortable than the tower where I normally worked, that seven-by-seven-foot box entered via trapdoor. A hummingbird feeder hung from one of the roof beams over the catwalk, and a bird bath at the base of the tower drew winged visitors that were fun to watch through binoculars, performing their adorable avian ablutions. A picnic table sat next to the bird bath, and beyond it a campfire ring and a stack of oak and pine: all in all a well-kept summer home.

Two metal sheds, a 250-gallon propane tank, an array of solar panels, and a radio-repeater tower dominated the south edge of the peak, next to the clearing for the helicopter LZ—more clutter than I would have cared for in a perfect world. But that was to be expected on a mountain to which you could both hike and drive. On the other hand, the road out brought you to the Buckhorn Saloon in Pinos Altos in approximately forty-five minutes if you hustled, the shortest travel time from tower to tavern of any lookout in the Gila. One evening I succumbed to the quitting-time allure of rolling down the mountain toward one of my friend Aari's impeccable dirty martinis, after which I raced back up the hill in time to catch the last of the twilight glow in the west, feeling a hint of a glow myself as I locked the gate behind me on the road.

John's presence permeated the 200 square feet of penthouse real estate where I cooked and slept and kept watch that June. Sometimes I had to leave the tower and wander around the mountain for twenty minutes just to get away from him. I was in that schizophrenic phase of grief where one minute I felt grateful for the chance to be close to him by inhabiting his space and engaging his view, walking in his footsteps as it were, and the next minute I felt a taunt from every little object he had once touched, each haunted by some residual immanence of him. He was there in the vase of plastic flowers set on the windowsill as an ironic gesture of suburban interior decoration. He was there in the bag of Smokey Bear lapel pins kept handy as swag for visitors with kids.

Even something as simple as a can of refried beans in the pantry had an evocative power, reminding me of our routine for Continental Divide Trail thru-hikers, those creatures of astounding stamina whose route brought them first to my mountain, then John's, on their journey from Mexico to Canada. By the time they reached me, they had traveled 130 miles through the desert—the bare beginnings of their 3,000-mile journey along the spine of the Rockies—and if they arrived after quitting time, I would share a swig of tequila with them in my tower as we looked upon the country they had traveled to get there and the route that lay ahead. Once they returned to the trail, either that same evening or the following morning, I would radio John and let him know that visitors were on their way, ETA twenty-four hours, give or take a couple, and he would do the prep work on a batch of homemade nachos in advance of their arrival the next day. We never met a thru-hiker who wasn't tickled by the gift economy of the Gila's southern sentinels: aperitif at my tower, appetizer at John's. All their sort had ever heard of the place were rumors of its rough beauty and its capacity for inflicting bodily punishment on those moving overland by foot, and here they were, being treated like visiting dignitaries and offered ritual sustenance on the very first peaks they ascended on their long trip north.

By the time I arrived on Signal Peak that season, the thru-hikers had all come and gone, and the surplus beans sat orphaned in the pantry. Probably they would remain there for years until some new lookout came along and threw them out, unacquainted with their history, unaware of their purpose.

ALTHOUGH I WAS SLOW TO REMEMBER the fact, it turned out I did still have John's voice in the form of the last phone message he left me. I saved it on the day after he hiked down the mountain with Teresa to avoid the heat and smoke of the Signal Fire. "Myself plus one will be departing for Highway 15 via the Signal Peak trail," he had informed the dispatcher by radio, just before setting off that afternoon. During the four weeks he had left to live, he teasingly called Teresa "Plus-one."

That evening I called him to offer my condolences. I knew

as well as anyone the divergent emotions John was feeling in the wake of his evacuation—the adrenaline high of the escape from an onrushing fire, swirled up with sadness at the thought of his cherished view forever transformed—and I wanted to remind him I had been there and welcome him to the club. When he didn't answer my call, I left him a message. The next day he called back and left one in turn. He joked that he now had a more dramatic chased-from-the-mountain story than mine, and teased me about a personalized copy of a gift I had given him, a book in which he made a brief appearance. He had been its earliest reader in manuscript form, and his enthusiasm for it, more than anything anyone later said or wrote by way of reaction, convinced me that the effort hadn't been in vain.

Once I rediscovered the message, I found myself dialing it up, alone at night in his tower, pressing the #4 key to repeat it on my phone's substandard speaker, the last words of his I would ever have, echoing in the last place he stood before he rode to his death. In any other season I would not have had the technology available to me, but that year, for the first time, Dennis required me to have a cell phone on the mountain. At first I resented this order. I had owned my sorry little flip phone for barely a year and didn't much care for it, its awkward presence in my life a reminder of my time as a couch-surfing bachelor who, suddenly lacking a fixed land line, still required a means of contact with realtors untangling marital commitments on my behalf. Eventually, though, I came to appreciate the communion it made possible. With every replay of John's last message I thought of his generosity, his laughter, his genius in the art of living boldly—and the rude injustice of his having checked out way too soon.

I thought too of the first time I heard him over the radio, twelve years earlier, when I was a raw rookie in the field of lookoutry and only knew him as a disembodied voice. I tried to picture him as he was then, a man just turned fifty years old, standing on the same catwalk where I now stood, staring out over the forest, his mind unsettled over Miquette's uncertain prognosis, unaware that in just a few months he would be standing there with her ashes in his hands.

"Hey Phil, what a nice message you left me yesterday. I came home and had to sit in the hot tub because, you know, I hiked down and loaded my pack with, well, your book, and that's what caused me to wrench my back, all that extra weight I had to load in. Also, Plus-one wants me to let you know that she says hi and sends her regards… Anyway, give me a call, and thanks again for the message… I'll repeat what you said in your inscription, and it was why I brought the book down the mountain with me, because you said I'll always be a cherished friend, and that's true of you too."

A MERE SIX WEEKS after he left me that phone message, my cherished friend inhabited a gallon Ziploc, and the moment had arrived for him to join with his mountain. Teresa unsealed the plastic bag. We dipped our hands in his cremains, extracted a pinch between our fingertips, let it float off below us toward a cluster of century plants. His ashes joined there with the ashes of the Signal Fire, his final form mingling with the final major burn to bloom on his watch. Within weeks, perhaps even days, a good rain would flush some of the ash and loose soil down the drainage, a nutrient recharge for the creek bottoms and, for a bit of his remnants, one last ride through a piece of country he had known better than anyone alive.

Sitting there alongside Teresa, a thin coating of grit on my fingers, grit that had once been the substance of a living man, I was surprised to find myself reminded of the Catholic masses of my childhood, when the priest, arms uplifted, would intone over the Eucharist the words of the doomed savior at his last supper: *Take this, all of you, and eat of it, for this is my body... Do this in memory of me.* John had been intimate with those same rituals. We had talked about how one is never quite a former Catholic, only a recovering one, the liturgy (and its obsession with sin) having been absorbed on an almost molecular level by our spongy young minds. For us, the metaphors had been more enduring than the faith, none more so than those of Ash Wednesday, when our foreheads had been traced by the priest's thumb, the cross-shaped smudge a reminder of mortality and mourning, a harbinger of what lay in store for us all:

For you are dust, and to dust you shall return...

Simultaneously, unprompted by word or gesture, Teresa and I both licked our fingers, wanting to take a bit of John into ourselves. I suppose some might view this as macabre, perhaps even a health hazard, but we had both inhaled the smoke of huge burns—as had John during his fifteen summers on the mountain—and the acrid bite of ash on the tongue was far from unfamiliar. The forests we had watched burn would evolve and become something else in time, spruce and fir succeeded by aspen, pine replaced by locust and oak, but what they had been was now, like John, a memento etched in flame.

As the heat of the day increased, a few proto-cumulus began

to form. Teresa and I tossed another pinch of John into the air, watched the motes twist and float on the breeze. We shared a bitter laugh at the irony of her having finally found, after decades of boyfriends and flings, a man she cared to stand by for the long run—only to have him maroon her at the altar in the most theatrical fashion possible.

"He did have a flair for the dramatic, didn't he?" she said. "It's really odd, but we took Sundance to the vet about a week before the accident. He'd been dropping his head every time he took a step with one of his legs, and we knew something was wrong, he was in some kind of pain. I told John it was probably the navicula in that hoof. I'd seen it before. Sure enough, after the exam the vet told us Sundance had navicular disease pretty bad. There wasn't much to be done about it. It was probably time to put him out to pasture."

She paused, shook her head as if trying to forget something or remember something, it was hard to say which.

"We were leaving the vet, and John was loading Sundance in the trailer. And he put his hand on the horse's muzzle and said, 'Well, looks like it's time for one last ride, my friend.' And wouldn't you know it, that's exactly what they did. John brought him here for that next hitch, and they both went for one last ride."

We both looked away, unable to maintain eye contact unclouded by tears.

"There's still so much I want to ask him, so much I want to know. I was looking forward to our airplane-joy-ride jaunt around the West. Only John could think of something so extravagant, golfing every day in a different state. It was the goofiest idea I'd ever heard for a honeymoon. How could I say no?"

She lifted the Ziploc bag and looked at it with a rueful smile that appeared, under the circumstances, an act of gallantry.

"Now it's just gonna have to be a road trip with these. I think I can probably find the secret valley in California where he used to camp with Miquette—or at least have a nice time trying. He took some of her ashes there. I feel like I should do the same for him. They ought to be together. And maybe you can take some to your mountain when you go back. Jean should have some too, up on her mountain. I've got some other places in mind that I know he liked. But sorry, buddy"—she glanced down at her hands—"none of them involve a putting green."

I laughed. We hugged each other, and she set off down the trail, back toward the home she had too briefly shared with John, where she would spend the next three years in a longer and more complicated relationship with his things—the Pantera, the GT40, the Cessna Cardinal, the BMW motorcyle, the 40-foot "land yacht," the list went on and on—than she had with the man himself.

MY RELATIONSHIP with John's memory also grew more complex as time passed. I began to wonder why he remained, in some inexplicable way, elusive to me—remains elusive even in this attempt to evoke him, as I'm sure is sadly evident by now, a pall of failure hanging over the entire effort. Rebecca Solnit articulated the feeling for me in a book published the year of John's death: *There is so much we don't know, and to write truthfully about a life, your own or your mother's, or a celebrated figure's, an event, a crisis, another culture is to engage repeatedly with those patches of darkness, those nights of history, those places of unknowing.* Sometimes John appeared in danger of being swallowed by the unknowing. I couldn't figure out how to engage with it short of fictionalizing—and that struck me as a potential desecration of his life.

John had made the effort to know me, perhaps even made it a little too vigorously for my taste. His relentless style of questioning often left scant room for reciprocal questions, although he freely shared of himself as he spilled confessional stories on the theory that confession breeds confession. I had taken John's confessions, he had taken mine, and they had deepened our understanding of each other's psychic weather and built a bridge of trust and care. But of course a man is more than the sum of his sins and regrets. So often those were what we confessed, like the Catholic boys we could not escape being.

It may have been the case that two fire lookouts, solitary by nature, could only ever know so much of each other's individuality. When we weren't confessing, much of the talk we shared revolved around work: goofball hikers and wicked weather, visits from bears and deer, our different vantages on seasons of smoke in the sky, the sort of singular experiences that bond members of an elite club. And the flip side of the old Catholic habit of confession is a penchant for secrecy, withholding, sleights of hand, the ongoing act of carving out shadowed space in one's life in a rebellious act of self-assertion, or perhaps self-protection, or both. In one of our conversations, we had discovered that we each first learned to lie the old-fashioned way, by being forced to confess our sins to a priest. What seven- or eight-year-old boy in his right mind would willingly cough up his real misdeeds to a paternal figure on the other side of a dark partition? It was the easiest thing in the world to make up less damning substitutes.

We had shared a great deal concerning our respective pasts. I don't believe we ever told each other a lie. I belatedly acknowledged that we must have withheld at least as much as we shared. I know I had. Only a sociopath would offer up his entire, unedited self to a friend for inspection. A part of me felt the impulse to track down people who had known him, question them for what they remembered of him, see what details I could ferret out to fill in the missing pieces of the puzzle, the pieces he had shielded from me, or simply not got around to sharing. But in a way I could not exactly articulate, I thought this might dishonor the friendship we had forged.

Or maybe I was just scared off because I had undertaken such a project on the life of my brother, sifting the wreckage of his suicide, hunting the secrets, and I didn't want to repeat the process. Once was enough. It was too spooky, with too many booby traps lying in wait. John made so many connections, showing different versions of himself to different people. A few of them sought me out after I eulogized him in the local newspaper, to tell me he had touched them in some way. It felt appropriate to allow those connections to spark or scatter as they would, unhunted by my forensic snooping into his many facets. Just as we would scatter his ashes here and there. Just as I would one day be scattered too.

IT WOULD TAKE ME another two years, but I did eventually go poking into the story of the kids and the plane crash, and the perils appeared immediately. Everyone I talked to had a view on the what and why of it, and half the people I reached out to told me they just couldn't talk about it. More than one person warned me against writing about it at all. It remained an emotional live wire, and even some who were willing to open up came to view me as a vulture or a voyeur, despite my effort to proceed with sensitivity. Who am I to say they were wrong? It has been the fate of more than one man to become rather too obsessed with death when, in the middle of the journey, he enters a dark wood.

A few conversations with friends and acquaintances were all it took to reveal that people's judgments on the crash were visceral, vehement, and largely dependent on pre-existing relationships. Some believed the crash a fluke of bad weather and bad timing and bad luck, and any suggestion to the contrary a vindictive effort to isolate a scapegoat. Others believed the crash a preventable mistake because the flight itself was a preventable mistake: arranged outside a structure of oversight that might have provided some check on its improvisational nature, and instigated by men who acted more from the dictates of their own egos than from concern for the safety of other people's children. In the messy struggle over the tragedy's meaning, there was a tendency for people to end up crouched in postures of mutual mistrust.

Given the nature of the mission—not just the flight but the mission of the school more generally—the crash raised questions about the risks associated with experiential learning, and whether the school had the right procedures in place to manage those risks. In one of the first official statements about the crash, a school administrator insisted that the flight was "not a school-sponsored trip." To many people, me included, those words had a funny smell to them.

The flight had been arranged on school grounds, by a teacher, in order to further a school project for which the students received a letter grade and internship credit. None of that was in dispute.

To say that the flight had not been "sponsored" by the school may have been technically accurate—but one could argue that was precisely the problem.

The very nature of experiential education requires heightened vigilance. Allowing kids experiences in the world inherently carries more risk than lecturing at them in a classroom. Given the increased risk of, say, a backpacking trip in the Wilderness—an annual ritual at the school and one that had gone awry more than once, when kids got lost after separating from their chaperone or got trapped on the wrong side of the river by floodwaters—teachers and administrators had a joint obligation to weigh the dangers and seek ways to minimize them.

Risk can never be eliminated, of course, nor would we want it to be. Most experiences worth having risk something, even if it's just our pride or our comfort. But in the realm of experiential education done by the book, it was far from ideal for one teacher to plan an outing in the morning and execute it that same afternoon, without any oversight by others, when among the risks of the outing was death.

In a different world, all the principal parties might have come together and engaged in a good-faith attempt to understand what had happened, and why, in the crash that took four lives. The school might have taken the lead, initiating an effort by which everyone involved sought to understand everyone else, and all shouldered a measure of responsibility, of varying heft. People skilled in directing such efforts—professional conflict mediators—existed in the community, but their expertise was not called upon, because we do not live in that world. We live in a world of liability insurance, "forward-thinking solutions," and lawyers who work in an adversarial system of justice. We live in a world where to admit a mistake is to unilaterally disarm in the struggle for control of the narrative.

By appearing to distance themselves from the crash, school officials gave an impression that, as one person with long association there told me, "they didn't want to autopsy the accident, they wanted to tweak their policies to avoid future accidents," as if those two things could be decoupled. The three sets of parents would come to the conclusion that they had no choice but to sue, in order to ensure that painful but necessary autopsy.

In settling the case before it went to trial, aware the outcome was a foregone conclusion, the school agreed to pay the maximum allowable under state law: $750,000 split equally among the families of the children. The estate of Dr. Hochla paid an additional, undisclosed sum. The school also issued a letter of reprimand to Steve Blake; offered a formal apology to the families, acknowledging the school's failure to vet the flight; and agreed to an examination of its risk-management policies by an outside professional.

For the parents, it hadn't been about vengeance. They cared about the school. They believed in experiential education. Even after the accident, the Mahls intended to enroll the youngest of their three sons there. Above all, they wanted an assurance that the experiences he would be offered had been carefully thought through ahead of time.

In my reading of the depositions generated by the lawsuit, the fundamental question appeared to revolve around a case of mission-completion bias that started long before Dr. Hochla tried to land his plane. The mission took on a sense of urgency for several reasons, including denial by the Forest Service of the eco-monitors' other attempts to see the burn—but mostly because it was the very last day of the school year. With time to mull it over, assess the risks involved, and consider various options, school personnel might have chosen a charter company that specialized in such trips. That would have offered them the assurance of a plane and a pilot subjected to—in the words of the commercial pilot Don Lewis—*rigorous maintenance requirements, training standards, proficiency requirements, a mandatory drug testing program, and safety management system*, the gold standard for taking private citizens on sight-seeing missions.

Even if they had opted to use Dr. Hochla and his plane, it would have been vastly preferable for more than one person to oversee the details of the flight. Dr. Hochla and Steve Blake had promised the parents they would cancel if the weather turned bad, which it did. Steve Blake deferred to Dr. Hochla's judgment that the weather was good enough; Dr. Hochla was the pilot, after all. But involving others with a less personal attachment to the pilot might have prevented the plane from ever leaving the ground with those kids aboard.

I dreaded reaching out to Blake, a feeling reinforced when the first three people I asked refused to share his phone number with me. Those closest to him formed a protective circle after the crash, so I only heard about him secondhand, and anyway I feared I knew too well his situation, for I had once lived it myself: that of the man who had found himself guilty of a crime of neglect and was living out a sentence that denied him a parole into happiness.

Four weeks before her death, Ella Myers wrote in her eco-monitor journal: *This year Steve taught me probably one of the most important lessons there is without even really meaning to. I came to realize from observation that Steve is a truly happy person. This is something quite rare indeed. He doesn't look for external happiness in the products we buy, or the people we surround ourselves with, nor the place where we are… No, it's a happiness that extends from within, and this happiness, though very hard to find, is often the most fulfilling.*

Since this realization, I've made it a priority to stop my endless searching for external happiness and realize that I'm alive… experiencing the insanity of a reality shaped by the ones within it.

This is perhaps one of the greatest lessons of all. Thank you Steve.

Those words echoed others I had heard about just how much Blake had been respected and loved by his students.

When I did finally call and schedule a visit, Blake graciously welcomed me into his home for a beautiful dinner of roasted chicken and salad with homemade mozzarella, courtesy of his wife, Denise. Afterward he led me on a hike out his back door, into the foothills of the Pinos Altos Range, that place of death and solace both. He told me that he alone took responsibility for the decision to put the kids on that plane, and that it still haunted him every single day. "You go through life thinking you're a force for good, a net positive in the world, working with students, mentoring them, and then one day you wake up and realize you might never get back to zero," he said. He had grappled with the sort of regret most of us cannot imagine, been on a journey whose contours we can only guess. His dreams, at least the ones he remembered, could not stop replaying images of airplanes.

If I had been John I'd have given him a hug, but we both knew the reason I was there. For the sake of a partial accounting of events in the life of the place we called home, I was going to expose to a community of readers the one decision in his own life he wished he could undo. I felt terrible about this, but he made no complaint—and even appeared to view our awkward meeting as the potential beginning of a friendship, not merely a one-off dictated by my sense of professional courtesy. "Nothing you write can make me feel worse than I already have," he said. "Tell the story your own way and let the chips fall where they will. And come back any time. I'm always up for a hike."

RATHER THAN ATTEMPT to resurrect John with words, I resolved to cultivate my connections with the living, and perhaps to our mutual surprise, much of that energy flowed toward Teresa and was returned in kind. For both of us the two years after John's death would be filled with trials both physical and, for lack of a better word, spiritual, and through it all we were never out of touch—indeed only grew closer as friends. She tore up her knee in a way that laid her low for months and led her to seek out a series of extremely uncomfortable injections of her own platelet-rich blood plasma in order to stimulate a healing response and avoid surgery, an effort that merely delayed the inevitable. The Cessna turned out to require complicated and expensive maintenance to make it sale-ready. And just to make life extra interesting, the engine in the GT40 blew up while a prospective buyer took it for a spin.

She handled all of this with her customary wry good humor, which is more than I can say for myself during my ordeals. As she bushwacked her way through a thicket of doctor's appointments and mechanic's consultations, becoming acquainted with all that was damaged in her own body and in John's toys, I embarked, the winter after John's death, on a 3,200-mile book tour by car, during which I broke the record for the saddest event in the history of bookstore events: a half-dozen people weeping in their folding chairs at a chain store in Las Cruces, New Mexico. For reasons both contextual and aesthetic—dreary mall anchor store, metal folding chairs arrayed in pitiful rows of three—I chose, on that particular night, to avoid reading one of the funny bits from my book about life in the shadow of my brother's suicide. Instead I went all in on the heavy stuff and got what I deserved: six people in tears and a new standard for the most lugubrious event in the annals of memoir marketing. A makeshift memorial or perhaps a single scented candle should mark the spot.

I could have shrugged off this indignity without any permanent injury to my psyche, but real injury was added to insult when I suffered a debilitating hip condition as a result of driving a distance equal to that of San Diego to New York in a cramped rental car on my suicide book tour. Immediately after it was over, I found that any sort of movement of my lower body induced a feeling like drywall screws were being turned very slowly in my groin. Unable to walk without pain, much less hike with a pack on my back, I rode to my lookout that spring on a horse, spent one month there, then rode back out when it became clear I was not going to heal spontaneously.

I spent the rest of the season on Signal Peak, since it was reachable by vehicle. On the one-year anniversary of John's death, once again performing my corrupt imitation of him, I felt angry and disconsolate, like a shell of a man—and the one man who would have listened and understood was gone forever.

That winter I underwent two surgeries of my own, first on the left hip, then the right, to repair a torn labrum and remove a bone spur in each. The operations laid me up for months and forced me to miss a summer in a fire tower for the first time in fifteen years.

Aside from Mónica's, Teresa's words of commiseration and encouragement were about the only ones that penetrated my fugue of self-pity, perhaps because she was so honest about her own struggles. *Finally cleaned out John's wallet yesterday after 21 months of keeping it around,* she wrote me in an email. *His license to fly, his credit card, a code to some gate scribbled on a scrap of paper. I'll keep it a bit longer because the leather is embossed with his body print. I still feel him as a shadow partner. We sit companionably in the hot tub together with the snow all around. I don't feel a need to speak to him out loud and break the silence of the dark sky, rosy in the east from the town lights. He talks to me through the heat of the water, and I see him when I look up from my book to trace the white line of snow down an oak branch that he arranged so gracefully with his pruning. I also came across some pictures from a time when we went hiking and found some closely spaced piles of bear shit. I think we counted 25 piles. I tilted my pants down, exposing my butt over one pile, claiming it as my achievement, a scrap of TP in my hand. He could barely hold himself together to snap the shot, and I can barely hold myself together when I think of it.*

Teresa not only hung in with me as I wrestled with chronic pain of the sort that resurrected the idea of a goodbye kiss with the mouth of my shotgun, she also indulged my half-serious jokes about the impulse toward self-murder. "You might want to try sacrificing a chicken first," she said. "And if that doesn't work, procreate and offer up your firstborn. And if that doesn't work, a hose from the exhaust pipe through the rear window of your truck is a lot less messy than a 12-gauge."

Once I finally felt well enough to travel again—after a year of being housebound—Teresa was there with an offer to drive me out into the mountains, to visit old haunts and reconnect with places that sustained us. We talked for hours as we meandered in the Mercedes Sprinter van she had lived in for twelve years prior to meeting John. Among other stories, she told me how she had become the first seasonal Forest Service employee ever to win a whistleblower case against her superiors through the White House Office of Special Counsel. It was a case she felt compelled to pursue after some clueless ranger on the Boise National Forest tried to have the guy-wire cables removed from her lookout. This was to be done for aesthetic reasons, an asinine idea that would have weakened the structural integrity of the wind-battered tower where she lived and worked at the edge of a steep cliff. She raised a stink to prevent a dangerous mistake and was fired for it. Like John, she was unafraid of confronting misguided authority, consequences be damned.

A bracing directness defined her demeanor, but if you listened carefully you learned that she often communicated on more than one level at once. Two days before my second hip surgery, for instance, she sent me a brief note and a link to a scientific paper. *Well, if it ain't one thing it's your mother. I know you are girding your loins for the upcoming event, but I thought you might be interested in this. Buena suerte. Break a leg. But I guess you already did that, didn't you? Unbreak it, then.*

The paper, published in the journal *BMC Biology*, detailed the discovery and classification of a group of organic compounds known by the common name "karrikins." The name was derived from an indigenous word for smoke, *karrik*, used by the Aboriginal Noongar people of western Australia. These compounds, made up of carbon, hydrogen, and oxygen, were produced when plant sugars burned. Vaporized and transported in smoke, the compounds eventually bound with surface soil particles. The first subsequent rains helped them percolate into the ground, bringing them into contact with long dormant seeds, which responded to the signal by germinating en masse.

The discovery of karrikins provided yet more evidence of a fact long known: that in the words of the study's authors, *plants have not only learned to live with fire, but also to exploit it.* And not just fire—also the chemical properties of smoke. This represented a surprising and, to my mind, beautiful addition to our understanding of nature's ways of communication. It also gave new meaning to the phrase "smoke signal."

Teresa and I were both wildfire geeks. She knew I had an amateur's interest in fire research. But I sensed, beneath the facade of her jocular note, another message on a different frequency, something more than an invitation to share in the fruits of scientific inquiry conducted with the aid of liquid chromotography and bioassay-guided fractionation. Aware of how long and discouraging a battle with chronic pain I had waged—how my faulty hips had robbed me of nearly every pleasure that previously sustained me— she seemed to offer access to a useful metaphor. *Something will grow from this, even though the landscape looks bleak. Something, even now, is being triggered to flower from the ruins.* Those, at any rate, were the unspoken words I chose to hear.

It cannot have been a coincidence that around that time, bedbound with nothing better to do, I began writing this story in earnest—the idea of karrikins acting as a sort of mental karrikin on my dormant urge to spin meaning out of the chaos of life.

But I see I've gotten ahead of myself once again, leaping forward in time from that morning when Teresa's departure from the mountain with a bag of John's ashes left me alone to the gathering spectacle in the sky. And what a spectacle: the ancient drama of the season's first monsoon moisture streaming north from the Gulf of Mexico, meeting the cauldron of the desert and rising over the mountains, the resulting cumulus clusters expanding and climbing, blowing up like popcorn kernels, their bottoms slowly darkening and the first tendrils of virga beginning to fall like the delicate strings of a beaded curtain, and finally the first hot flash of a ground strike in the middle distance, then another, and another. By midafternoon dry lightning jabbed the mesas to the north every few seconds. New smokes were popping up, demanding my attention. I called in three in the span of an hour. Still unfamiliar with the terrain from John's vantage point, I misplaced one of them by two miles. The crew sent to suppress it found it anyway by talking me through the landmarks and flashing a signal mirror in my direction.

That evening, off the clock and out of service, I took a couple of pulls off the tequila bottle John had left behind. Then I rinsed my mouth, uncapped his tube of lipstick, and made myself up in the reflection of his signal mirror. As I stood on the catwalk in the day's last light, lips puckered, a sad clown waiting on a hummingbird's kiss, I couldn't help thinking that the man I would have liked to ask about the contours of the landscape, the man who better than anyone could have alleviated my ignorance, was forever out of service. No longer up above the country keeping watch, he was now a part of it—and a part of me.

〰〰〰〰

A MONTH OF WORKING John's shifts on Signal Peak, once it was over, felt like plenty long enough in his space. His relief lookout, Mark Johnson, would take over for what remained of the season, and Mark's boss Keith Matthes would spell Mark for a day off now and then. I was more than happy to step aside. They had both been close with John, each in his own way closer than me, and it felt right to leave the place in their hands. Besides, I had fallen into a trap that sometimes snares the grieving. Alone, I found the dead were more alive to me than the living. The living moved like shadows on the periphery of a dream where the dead lived again. But of course the dream could not last.

It wasn't just John I kept alive in my imagination, but those three Aldo Leopold Charter School students. My inner ear kept playing a remembered moment from that open-mic event at Diane's Parlor, two months before the plane crash, when Michael Mahl sang Leonard Cohen's "Hallelujah" with a haunting beauty that made my skin tingle. I often remembered the poignant last words he posted to social media on the occasion of his sixteenth birthday, less than two weeks before he died: *I'm so thankful for everyone in my life and there is not a single thing or person that I take for granted. Thanks everyone for the birthday wishes. It's been the greatest 16 years I could ask for. I have treasured the good moments, embraced the love, and cherished a life well lived.*

My thoughts also turned to Ella Myers and all the writing that ought to have been still ahead of her, a prize-winning author by the age of sixteen, a young woman who emanated intelligence and curiosity even through the scrim of her shyness, and whose closest companion had been her horse. *I wish that time could halt,* she had once written. *That moments in our lives where we find happiness could last forever… I wish I could drive out all the darkness in our world and leave only light… But most of all I wish that somehow, some way, I shall leave something behind long after I am gone.* After her death I learned from her mother that she had carried around like a talisman a book I had inscribed to her, *one writer to another,* by way of encouragement. The world felt crueler for the fact that she had not lived long enough to return the favor, but her words nonetheless lived on in the memories of those who had read them.

I thought as well of Ella Jaz's efforts in defense of the Gila River, and that petition with 6,470 signatures she delivered to the governor, asking for a reprieve from the diversion dam that made the river as much a source of worry as delight for those of us inclined to care about things wild and free. Having felt an urge to bend my sorrow to some redeeming purpose, I had turned my creative energies toward preventing a foreseeable death: the death of the river below the dam. My efforts were exceedingly modest, I admit. They mostly involved writing a regular column for the local newspaper at $25 a pop, a column in which I attempted to channel the voices of John and Ella Jaz in order to throw light on the shenanigans of those who dreamed of destroying the river. I was guided too—as usual—by a nugget of wisdom from Aldo Leopold: *Somehow the watercourse is to dry country what the face is to human beauty. Mutilate it and the whole is gone… The economist, the engineer, or the forester may feel there has been no great loss and adduce statistics of production to prove it. But there are those who know, nevertheless, that a great wrong has been committed—perhaps the greatest of all wrongs.*

Despite more than a century's worth of ideas to dam it near its headwaters, the stream still ran unmolested through about as rough and broken a piece of country as you could find in the continental US, the southern portion of the Gila Wilderness. The difficult topography was a big part of what had saved it from the engineers and boosters down the decades. But their tools had only gotten bigger, and if the bureaucrats at the Interstate Stream Commission (ISC) in Santa Fe had their way, the moment the river escaped from its mountain fortress and crossed the Wilderness boundary into the Gila-Cliff valley, it would at last be tamed and made servile to man, at a projected cost of more than a billion dollars.

The back story was complicated, as water law tends to be in the West, but the short version could be summarized by reference to the novelist and poet Jim Harrison, who once wrote: *Man has an inexhaustible ability to beshit his environment, with politicians well in the lead.* In 2004, Congress passed the Arizona Water Settlements Act (AWSA), which dealt with numerous water-rights issues in the state. In a bit of horse-trading necessary to win support for the bill from New Mexico senators Pete Domenici and Jeff Bingaman—both of them crucial votes on the Senate Committee on Energy and Natural Resources—the Arizona delegation agreed to throw in some additional money for water projects in the four counties of southwest New Mexico. Congress authorized $66 million for that purpose. It also stipulated—and this is the crucial detail—an additional amount up to $62 million be made available if the state opted to construct a diversion dam on the Gila River.

That dangling carrot skewed the incentives in predictable

ways. The $66 million could have been spent on conservation and watershed restoration, effluent reuse and upgrades to existing infrastructure—proven, cost-effective ways of addressing water demand. The state could have left the $62 million on the table and said no thanks to another disaster of industrial ingenuity. But that's not how Western water politics works. First comes the solution—almost always a dam—and then follows the search for a problem to justify it.

But there was no problem. Farmers in the Gila-Cliff valley already took all the water they needed with a temporary earthen diversion rebuilt in the river each spring. "We don't have a shortage of water," one local expert told me. "We have an excess of money encouraging us to do something stupid."

The river Ella Jaz knew—the river Ella Myers and Michael Mahl and John knew too—was unrecognizable in engineering studies I read that summer at the tower after hours. In one fever dream the majority of the river's flow would be diverted through a nine-foot-diameter pipe blasted through a mountain and aimed into a stagnant side-canyon reservoir. Certain parties of an exceptionally grandiose temper argued for the water to be pumped from there up and over the Continental Divide and sluiced through a pipeline seventy miles to the dusty little burg of Deming.

The studies were bought and paid for by the ISC, then obligingly churned out by its favored hirelings in the engineering-consulting racket. The engineers mostly portrayed the river as an underutilized ditch that—if repurposed for "wiser use" than simply letting a river go about the business of being a river—could slake the thirst of citizens in another river basin entirely, lure new industries to an artificial oasis in the desert, and provide additional irrigation options to a few dozen hobby farmers, all with welfare water paid for by someone else. A diversion dam was theoretically possible. Therefore the engineers had an obligation to play with the idea in the sandbox of their imaginations. But their dream was so brazenly irresponsible that to criticize it on technical or scientific grounds felt like trying to wound a hippopotamus with a pellet gun.

If you looked hard enough through the blizzard of acronyms and jargon, the smoke and mirrors of grandiose proposals, you found a simple motivation and a sly strategy. The strategy appeared to be to conjure the most byzantine plan imaginable, as profligate as possible, so that when it had to be scaled back to jibe with fiscal reality, the plan's authors could pat themselves on the back for their prudence and responsibility. The motivating impulse arose out of an old grudge. The goal, stated baldly by more than one dam proponent, was to do whatever it took to prevent Gila River water from crossing the state line to Arizona. New Mexico officials had long cultivated the fiction that the state had been stiffed in the water wars of the 20th century. Now it was payback time, and the Gila would have to be placed upon a sacrificial altar to settle old scores.

The intellectual contortions required to buttress the dream were a thing to behold. One report ginned up by the consultants claimed a diversion dam had the potential to *increase* habitat for an endangered minnow species downstream. That's right: re-engineer and de-water the river they've called home for millennia, and they'll thrive like never before! Meanwhile the real story was revealed by a close inspection of public records, which turned up back-channel text messages between a local water commissioner angling to oversee the project and an investment banker in Denver eager to make a "bankable deal."

It will come as no great news flash if I take a moment to note that a lust for domination over nature comes part and parcel with other forms of dominance. Paying witness to the personalities most invested in the whole charade revealed that the ISC bureaucrat who pushed hardest for a dam—indeed without whose chicanery the idea would have died in the cradle—was the sort of man who made a habit of bullying employees and belittling opponents. Court documents I dug up in Santa Fe revealed that the state had quietly settled a lawsuit that detailed his pattern of racial harassment of an ISC subordinate. This same man had also, with no trace of shame, once called the upper Gila River "the G-spot of New Mexico" in an open public meeting. If, in his wet dreams, the river was akin to female genitalia, then it didn't take a Freudian to figure out what was represented by the big hard piece of concrete that would violate it.

The US Department of Interior would have the final say on the dam's feasibility and compliance with environmental laws. Congress mandated that a "record of decision" be handed down by the feds by the end of 2019. If history was any guide, politics could massage the outcome either way, science and fiscal responsibility be damned. In the meantime I resented having to sit through Orwellian public meetings in order to come to grips with the sort of hubris and dishonesty that could call the whole thing—and with a straight face—*ecologically beneficial*. The upper Gila watershed was home to seven threatened and endangered species of fish, birds, frogs, and snakes. With a diversion dam stealing water from the river, it would be robbed of the natural pulses of energy and nutrients that made it a living system—the ebb and flow that continually reshaped the floodplain and rejuvenated niche habitats crucial to those creatures' survival. None of this troubled the schemers and dreamers. By their reckoning the fish would somehow survive in a river without water. The cottonwoods that offered nesting habitat to the birds would somehow learn to drink sand.

For those who followed every serpentine twist and turn in the process, there was one inescapable conclusion. The water buffaloes were in the grip of a religious delusion. Who would pony up the $900 million shortfall once the $128 million promised by the feds ran out? If any of them knew they weren't saying. Exactly how much water would the project yield? They couldn't be bothered to share the numbers. Who were the precise end users of the water? Their identities changed month to month. Would the proposed reservoir site hold water or leak like a sieve? The question was of zero interest, since the engineers had a foolproof plan to line the thing with an enormous plastic diaper. What would happen as global warming inevitably diminished the river's flow? Merely to mention it marked you as the dupe of a left-wing hoax.

It was an axiom oft proven in the West that when water law put the fate of a river in the hands of bureaucrats, engineers, and investment bankers, they could find a way to make it flow uphill toward money. Contemptuous of dissent, impatient with nettlesome questions, these men—and they were almost without exception men—turned in their rhetoric with surprising frequency to mention of forebears and forefathers. They appeared intent on summoning in the imagination the sort of hard-handed go-getters who dug the first irrigation ditches with steam shovels more than a century ago, not to mention extirpated the wolves and grizzlies from some of the roughest country in the Lower 48, to make it safe for civilization and beef cattle, though not in that order. Even as they tipped their caps to a mythologized past, they insisted it was the prosperity of future generations that mattered above all—and the future would assess their character by one criterion only. They would be judged by whether or not they had shown the *cojones* to stick a straw in the state's last wild river and suck.

Their recall of history tended to be highly selective, as is always the case with demagogues and fantasists. They failed to mention, for instance, the most renowned forefather of all, the godfather of the Gila Wilderness, Aldo Leopold. When he first came to the country in 1909, a newly minted forester fresh out of Yale, he found six mountainous areas in New Mexico and Arizona with more than half a million roadless acres at their core. A decade later all but one—the headwaters of the Gila River—had been splintered by roads. It was a moment of reckoning in our treatment of wild places, and Leopold seized the chance to protect one last big remnant of our natural heritage in the Southwest.

The parallels to the present reckoning could hardly be missed. Once again, the Gila encompassed the last of something—in this case, the state's last free-flowing river. Every other main-stem stream in New Mexico was subdued by human infrastructure, dammed for agricultural and municipal water, backed up in bathtub reservoirs beloved by jet skiers and bass fishermen. The state's most storied river, the Rio Grande, was a dessicated swath of sand in long stretches across its middle for much of each year. That stood in stark contrast with the Gila, which even the engineers who prepared the preliminary report on a diversion dam acknowledged as still "wild and scenic"—for now.

There was another vision for the future of the river, one articulated in the advocacy and writings of Ella Jaz: a precious ribbon of riparian lushness, a haven for fish and wildlife, and a variable but unending song of celebration for the miracle of flowing water in the desert. Hers was the truer vision, by far the more beautiful one, and the one destined to prevail if science, common sense, and humility were brought to bear in the final analysis. *Water has always been the difference between life and death, boom or bust, and it will be the difference once again between a sustainable future and no future at all,* she had written. *Though it may be hard to transition to a sustainable lifestyle of limited growth and renewable resources, it's mandatory if we want to continue on this planet for a little while longer and leave this good Earth alive, after we are gone.*

It was her farsighted perspective that I chose to celebrate when the first monsoon storms sent a pulse of floodwater down the canyons that summer, coincidentally on my days off from the tower. For years I had devoted myself to a study of the ways of fire, but I sensed a new obsession beginning to percolate—the ways of water, which were intricately linked with the ways of fire, since the forest of the high country determined the character of the watershed. The vegetation and soils of the mountains having undergone a radical realignment due to the big burns, so too would the river in the years to come. It would see muddier and flashier floods, for example, with less forest litter to hold the soil in place in the headwaters, and the spring runoff would begin much earlier, with far less shade on the snow of the high peaks to hold it in place.

One way to begin to understand a watershed is to be on the

water as it sheds. Besides, it was past time to visit the scene of the premeditated crime, in honor of Ella Jaz's efforts to forestall that crime. So I packed up my inflatable kayak and a few necessary supplies and threw them in the back of my truck. The Wilderness run—a run I had long imagined but not yet attempted—beckoned.

MÓNICA JOINED ME for the journey, which was only appropriate, since the purpose involved not merely homage to a wild river, but celebration of my recovered ability to sit for long stretches in a boat or anywhere else for that matter, an ability I owed entirely to her. Many a therapy session was required to bring about this miracle, but she never blanched at her role in my revival as a fully functioning human being. In fact she embraced it. The bestowal of nicknames began not with me calling her Lady Magic Finger, but with her calling the gland in question her Little Friend. It was a bold move, adopting the most damaged part of me as something to be cherished and tended to. She typically performed her remedial treatments on said amigo to the accompaniment of lit candles and meditative music designed to create a mood of mental relaxation and sphincter acquiescence— the whole business yet another reminder of the messiness of the human animal, and real mountain man stuff, no doubt about it. Over time a procedure I viewed as a necessary indignity evolved into an occasion for teasing, laughter, and a surprisingly sweet sort of intimacy, the old story of one human helping another turn the unacceptable into a source of amusement and pleasure—another possible working definition of unconditional love.

How such a benighted creature—a gringo with a dubious prostate, a beat-up pickup truck, and no obvious prospects for career advancement in a line of work so archaic that each new season on the payroll of the US government felt like a small miracle—became the object of her affection is a question best left to philosophers of the human heart more perceptive and cutting-edge than me. I do know that our culture conditions us to believe in the existence of a person, often defined as a soul mate, who will reach inside of us and touch our most sensitive place without fear, and in so doing take away at least some measure of our hidden hurt. I had always looked on this idea as a fairy tale, as nourishing and manufactured as Velveeta cheese. Then it happened to me, and not metaphorically.

I was one of those people seemingly born with an autumnal hoarfrost on my soul, whereas it appeared always to be springtime in hers. She had a serenity about her I found enormously attractive. A bilingual native of the borderlands, she was a tenacious reporter and a gifted storyteller. She had the fluid identity that comes from straddling cultures, equally at home on both sides of the line—a dual citizen of the US and Mexico. (Her great-grandmother had become a US citizen at the age of 100, just in time to cast a vote in the 2000 presidential election, although she died before the final result was known.) Whenever we were together, we began the morning with *la hora Hispanica*, during which she spoke only Spanish and demanded I do the same. Verb conjugation bedeviled me, but I was a quick study of the language of the kitchen and the bedroom, realms where it behooved me to please.

Having shared with me some of her world, Mónica was game to see some of mine.

To her, growing up in El Paso, a river was an unloved, used-up thing, a channelized ditch lined with concrete and littered with trash. I felt compelled to show her it could be otherwise, just as she had shown me a different face of Ciudad Juárez than the one I read about in the papers: a port of passage coveted by competing drug syndicates, and a city mutilated by the blood sacrifice of its vulnerable young women.

It didn't hurt that she, like Teresa, was fearless. Or if not exactly fearless, then respectful of her fear but undeterred by it—brave, but not self-dramatizing about it. She had spent the early part of her career covering the cartel violence in Juárez, one of four journalists based in El Paso, all of them women, who dared cross the border and see the carnage for themselves. It hadn't made her cynical so much as grateful for the life she had, the accident of birth that placed her on the safer side of an arbitrary line that year by year grew more militarized, more politicized.

Having seen what she had seen in the streets of Juárez, the thought of a river trip didn't faze her at all. The entirety of her kayaking experience consisted of a ten-mile float along a calm stretch of the Rio Grande up near Taos a few months earlier—a Gila trip would more than quadruple that—and mine amounted to not that much more. I had run lower reaches of the river in previous years, but those were just afternoon jaunts through the Gila-Cliff valley, downstream of the proposed dam and hardly more than shouting distance from a road at any given time. All of which is to say that we were as green as the country after a month of monsoon rains, and that felt somehow fitting. The river would teach us the lessons we needed to learn, just as it had taught Ella Jaz and she had taught others.

I vaguely recalled someone telling me that the forty-two miles from the junction of the headwater forks to a takeout spot at

Mogollon Creek could be run in one epic day if the flow was right, although the usual method involved camping multiple nights along the way. I made a couple of phone calls, hoping to confirm this rumor lodged in some dark fissure of my cranium. Neither was answered. We decided to go gonzo style and leave the camping gear behind.

Dawn of a gray and misty morning found us cruising north on the dead-end pavement toward the put-in spot. The campground at the convergence of the forks was empty. The morning and the river were ours. We had hoped to be on the water by 8 a.m.— we had no way of knowing the precise time, as neither of us bothered to wear a watch—but it seemed a safe bet that the target hour had come and gone by the time the kayak was inflated, the sandwiches made, the dry bags packed. Then we were off, under the bridge and around the first bend, beyond sight of man-made infrastructure until the gauging station that measured the river's flow forty miles downstream.

An undisturbed river is as perfect a thing as we will ever know, Tom McGuane once wrote, *every refractive glide of cold water a glimpse of eternity.* I knew whereof he spoke. I had found it possible to slip outside of time while fishing or walking along the river, or by sitting on its banks and remaining silent in the presence of its murmured profundities. In a boat, though, moving with a river, all thoughts of eternity vanish. There is only the present moment, and constant calibrations with your paddle to stay pointed down the main channel, and recurring anticipation of the river's next movement, the next bend, the tricky chute, the eddy, the swirl. To be on a wild river in a boat is to snap to attention in the now.

We had our first kiss with whitewater sometime before

lunch—merely Class II, but nothing to sneeze at in my tippy little Sea Beagle—and not long afterward we got a glimpse of a fallen tree across the river up ahead. To get the animal juices flowing, you can hardly do better than to be forced to pull hard across the current of a swift-moving stream to the safety of an eddy when the main channel has every intention of slamming you into a huge, half-submerged sycamore with "widow-maker" written all over it. Sometimes we floated on a surface smooth as glass for a quarter mile, only to round a bend and find a sweeper, a strainer, or a run of submerged rocks whipping the water into a frothy, chocolate meringue.

Late in the afternoon we came hard and fast toward a cliff face in a dog-leg bend of the river. We failed to find the safety of the slow-moving water along the near bank, then failed to turn the boat parallel to the cliff. The bow T-boned the rock in a perfect wall shot, the stern swung downstream, and before we knew it the craft had capsized. We both went under and bobbed back up, spitting and gasping. Mónica grabbed the boat and one of our paddles. I lunged wildly for the other paddle and her hat. Nothing was lost, no one hurt, but we both felt it to have been the sort of rude baptism that brings into focus the prospect of a sudden, soggy death—an adrenaline jolt and an indelible memory if luck holds, as ours did.

We floated twelve hours without seeing a single human being, indeed little evidence of a human presence at all, aside from a few pictographs and an adobe granary mortared into cliff rock a thousand years earlier. I could not recall a time in my life when I felt more invigorated. The aura of danger can have that effect. But it was also the water, and the light on the water, and the sounds it made, and the felt presence of unseen creatures that shared it with us, the hellgrammites and stone flies, the canyon frogs and catfish, the minnows and suckers and chubs.

On one quiet stretch of water I looked up at the tiered mesas above us and felt it might be true that my life was both a fire *and* a river, depending on the moment and the vantage from which it was viewed—and never more like a river than in moments like this, when memories of the past and concern for the future drop away, and there is only a feeling of immersion in the flow of a singular place where, as Siddhartha said, *everything has existence and is present,* the living and the dead, the creatures winged and finned and furred, their voices all alive in the voice of the river and us blessed to share in the music of that choir.

By nightfall we hadn't made the takeout, as any sane person could have predicted. We bivouacked on a sandbar under some cottonwood trees, near where the boosters proposed to maim the canyon with backhoes and bulldozers. I lit a fire to dry out our clothes. We tucked ourselves in the boat side by side for warmth beneath the cold light of a gibbous moon. "You said this would be epic," Mónica reminded me, "but I don't think that word does it justice. It's loco what you gringos do for fun. But I think I might learn to like it."

Her sanguine demeanor did not surprise me; my overconfidence in my boatman's abilities went mercifully unmentioned. A down-canyon breeze rustled the leaves of the cottonwoods, and the hiss and splash of the water made sweet white noise to sleep by, if only fitfully. Sometime in the middle of the night, we agreed our next adventure ought to take us to Mexico, deep in the interior this time, to the high mountains of

Michoacán, where monarch butterflies overwintered on oyamel fir trees at the southern end of their migration. We had heard tell that when the sun warmed them in the afternoons, they took flight above the forest and colored the sky like floating pieces of stained glass, each one representing the soul of a deceased loved one in the lore of the region's indigenous people.

In the morning I sprinkled a bit of John's ashes in the river from the mouth of a plastic match case, knowing he would have appreciated the journey, hoping his presence in the flow might ward off evil designs on that flow. Then we shoved off and ran another five miles of gorgeous stream toward the takeout spot, five miles that, if the dipsomaniacs ever got their way, would never again hum with the energetic pulse of floodwater, but instead squalidly dessicate in the shadow of poured concrete and concertina wire.

We made several portages along the final stretch, not wishing to tangle with strainers and sweepers that littered the channel: a river doing its ancient thing, heedless of human designs.

Forever may it remain—a siren song of adventure to the curious, and a lesson in humility for those who still care to be humbled.

JOHN JOINED THE LIFE of two more mountains before the summer of his death was up. I hiked in to my tower for the last hitch of the season with the remainder of my personal portion of his ashes in that waterproof match case. It was good to be home again, and good to have him there with me. He had never visited while I occupied the mountain—our summer schedules typically coincided, making such a visit impossible—so I carried him around for a few days in my pocket, showing him all my favorite places, the high meadows and hidden springs, the stone grottos and arboreal chapels where I came closest to a feeling of spiritual devotion. By the time I finished the tour, I had nearly convinced myself that I had done it for his sake, not mine.

One evening after a thunderstorm, I carried the ashes into the meadow and sprinkled them in two separate huecos where the rains pooled. Frogs had emerged there again that summer, and it pleased me to think of a bit of John joining with the cycles of amphibian life: cycles of eating and breeding, death and rebirth.

It pleased me to think of him dissolving in water.

The mere scattering of ashes nonetheless felt insufficient. The moment called for something else, something liturgical, a secular catechism or incantation. I knew what I must do as soon as I had the thought, despite how goofy it would have appeared if anyone had stumbled up the trail and witnessed me in the midst of it. From the table in the cabin I retrieved my lookout's commonplace, the coffee-stained notebook where I transcribed passages from my reading on the mountain going back years. I brought it to the edge of the bigger pool in the meadow, where his ashes still swirled smokelike in the water, and sat down with it open on my lap. I cleared my throat and apologized in advance to the birds and declaimed in my most sonorous voice every appropriate entry, a mishmash song of celebration for all we had seen and known during our years on the peaks, a litany for lookoutry and solitude and Wilderness and wildfire, with lyrics courtesy of Stendhal and Camus and Doug Peacock and Jack Kerouac, Ellen Meloy and Rebecca Solnit, Freya Stark, Willa Cather, a few dozen others.

For instance, Norman Rush: *Infrared waves just below twenty hertz associated with approaching thunder seem to have strange effects*

on the temporal lobe in some part of the population, to wit producing
feelings of baseless awe and ecstasy.

The words of others, apropos though they were, nonetheless
felt slightly impersonal without a few words of my own. As the
crepuscular hour overtook the land below me, and the long views
receded until I was alone in a merging of shadows, I improvised
a direct address:

You were beautiful, John. I don't know how you became the
man you did—I think it was an act of pure self-invention, one
of the most remarkable I've ever seen the fruits of. You had every
reason to turn out as one of those emotionally autistic men we
grew up around in the native home of the passive-aggressive.
Instead you became the opposite of that. You tasted tragedy early,
too early, actually way too damn early, but as time passed you
found it in you to focus on what a lucky son of a gun you turned
out to be, how kissed by fortune your life ended up, and you
made it your mission to kiss a little of that fortune forward into
the lives of others. Yep, I just said son of a gun without thinking,
but I bet you would have laughed at the unintentional pun—you
son of a gun in more ways than one. You always got the joke.
You never hid your enthusiasm, never reined yourself in when
feeling ecstatic. Your first impulse was always to share, to give, to
seek understanding, and perhaps most crucially you never feared
appearing corny. How cloistered and crabbed most of us end up
for wanting to avoid looking corny! How pinched and stunted,
how armored in layers of irony, how diminished in our range
of responses to life. You couldn't tolerate such diminishment in
yourself, quite the opposite—your emotional life appeared always
to be growing and evolving. No one I know was more generous

with affection. I don't think I ever properly thanked you for that. I miss your hugs already, even though they sometimes made me uncomfortable, they went on so long and with such force. I miss your voice too. And those ice-blue eyes shining with mischief. It occurs to me now that you gave me two of the biggest thrills I've had in this part of the world. Each was an instance of what you called "white guys enjoying the fruits of peak oil," a nod to our ridiculous good fortune: the afternoon we went 130 miles an hour in the foothills of the Black Range in your GT40, and the morning we flew over the forest in your Cessna, buzzing every lookout tower just before the start of fire season as if to offer them all our blessing. Both times I almost puked from motion sickness, but I still remember them fondly. Just as I'll always remember you.

How's this for corny: I wish I had told you I loved you, John. Loved you like a brother. I hope you were able to sense that I did.

More than that, I wish I had loved you better.

I guess I'll try to stay thankful for having had the chance to know you at all.

OVER ON JEAN'S MOUNTAIN, a special delivery from Teresa, three hours by Jeep from Silver City—John's Jeep, of course, yet another of his many toys—first along the highway to the Mimbres valley, then up past the Wilderness ranger station and onto the rough and rutted path of the old stage coach route, down into one rocky canyon and back up out of it and down into another canyon and back up out of it, past the Fowler place all the way to the fire camp near Jack Diamond's ranch, and from there on toward the Turkey Track road and the trailhead that marked the beginning of two more hours to the mountain on foot, a portion of what was left of John arrived in a plastic sandwich bag. Jean's first thought, she later wrote to me, was this: *I don't think I rate. I don't deserve this honor.* Teresa insisted without explicitly insisting. She had worked that mountain herself for years, liked the idea of some of John hanging out there, and more importantly Jean had been a good friend. John had loved and admired her. He would have been pleased at the thought of a piece of himself delivered into the life of the place by her two hands.

In the previous year they had conducted an email back-and-forth spanning several months and more than 25,000 words—a more candid correspondence, on a wider variety of subjects, than Jean had carried on with anyone else ever—and a major thread of it involved their shared thoughts about vulnerability and courage. Their frankness turned the discussion into an actual performance of vulnerability and courage. Parts of it, when Jean later shared it with me, made me cry.

Among the many things that struck me was John's mention of the event that changed his life as a young man, which was part of a larger discussion about the human need for the intimacy of touch. *When I was 17, my friend Mark and I were in the woods tinkering with guns and Mark shot himself in the head. My dad picked me up from the police station afterwards without saying much, and when I got home, my mother turned her back on me as soon as I walked in the door… I felt so unloved and unlovable and angry and lost and alone.* So much would have been different, he thought, if only his parents had reacted not with disappointment but with empathy, and simply given him a hug. One had to admire the fact that he became such an unrestrained giver of them, making himself an ambassador for a thing of which he had been, at a crucial moment in his life, deprived.

Another passage struck me in their correspondence, this one from Jean: *I say yes to everyone. I don't have the courage to say no.* It was true. She had the classic Midwesterner's attribute of wanting to please everyone, to never cause a ruckus, never disappoint, and people sometimes took advantage of it. She couldn't help herself. It ran in the family. She was meticulous. She had a huge and sensitive heart, a fact she did her best to hide under a blanket of self-deprecation. She constantly examined whether she had done the right thing in a certain circumstance, constantly questioned her own motives—it was a trait both endearing and maddening because it made you want to shake her and tell her she was good people extraordinaire, when instead she found reason to doubt that fact every other hour of the day. With Teresa standing in front of her on the mountain, courage required her to say yes—as if she were capable of saying no in this instance, refusing a gift freely given, sending Teresa back down the hill without taking the bit of John measured out for precisely that place, precisely her hand.

Jean held onto the ashes, days turning into weeks while she avoided a moment she could not bring herself to confront. She had never spread anyone's ashes. She wasn't sure how to handle them. It was the sort of thing you pretty much had to get right on the first try. She needed to think it through. Bury some in the soil? Let them go with the wind? She couldn't quite settle on a plan. She didn't want to botch the most important ritual she had ever performed on her mountain.

Remembering that John had already been divided and scattered here and there, with further scatterings still to come, she realized there could be no harm in doing both: bury a little, scatter a little. She bided her time, waiting for just the right day. It kept not coming. *I'm really not one for ceremony*, she later admitted. *Too much Catholic for too long maybe.* (Amen, sister.) But she knew this called for whatever impulse toward ceremony she could still muster. She needed a fully formulated plan, a meaningful gesture, one she could reenact each year henceforth. Something to give form to the feeling in her chest. Something to signify how much John had meant to her, while at the same time honoring his spirit of irreverence. She stowed the ashes in a safe place in her tower, hiked out for a few days off, and when she returned she brought a can of Miller Lite, although she had stopped drinking on the mountain years earlier. Miller Lite: John's beer. She would share it with him. Some to the ground with his ashes, some for her so he wouldn't drink alone.

More than once she walked toward her favorite tree on the south side of the hill, looking out over the headwater forks of the river toward Signal Peak, a stretch of country Teresa liked to call "the navel of the world," having absorbed its many moods and mysteries during her years watching over it. That characterization felt apt once you saw the view yourself, a view the majesty of which made you believe the story that Geronimo had been born there, down where the river's forks came out of their separate canyons and merged—a place gnarly enough and beautiful enough to have delivered to the world a child who would become in time a legend.

Still the moment kept not feeling right. She would walk to the tree and stand there awhile and walk away with the ashes still in her hand. *Something was missing, I wasn't sure what.* Perhaps a certain mood, a certain congruence of weather and rite. *So I thought some more on it and decided that I wanted to wait for one of those really foggy days, the days when my mountain sits in the clouds and for me things seem a little magical, though magic isn't quite the right word.*

The day would come, she knew. Thirteen summers on high had taught her many things, that among them. A day would come, likely before the end of July, mid-August at the very latest, when she would lift her head from the pillow on her narrow single bed, next to the south-facing windows of her tower, and find herself swaddled in mist, having slept inside a cloud. The thrill of that never got old, no matter how many times it happened: waking on what felt like an island, the sky above blotted out by tufts of cotton candy and the land below drowned in seas of water vapor, the visible world—normally so vast, such a smorgasbord of delights for the landscape-enraptured—reduced to a handful of nearby trees and a hillock of earth caressed by tendrils of fog. Unable to see beyond a hundred yards in any direction. Unable to see Signal Peak except in her mind's eye, the protuberant bump of it on her southern horizon, from which John, just a few weeks earlier, had given her a flash with his signal mirror so she could calibrate her Firefinder precisely with his tower.

When that foggy day finally arrived, I took the Miller Lite and John's ashes and headed for the tree. I dug a little hole in the ground and poured some of the ashes in. I said some words—a goodbye, an I'll miss you, a promise to make it an annual ceremony. Some of the beer went with him into the ground, some of it went to me. Then I climbed the tower. The wind had picked up a bit, enough to carry some of the ashes away with it, and I let the remaining ashes fall from the window.

It was an east wind, as it usually is when the monsoon plume flows northwest from the Gulf of Mexico and a back door cold front pushes across the low country of the Rio Grande rift. The ashes drifted westward from the tower, to a spot that marked the uppermost reach of the canyon running away below her. With the rainy season about to set in for real, perhaps a few molecules would hitch a ride on moving water, dribbling downhill, a few feet at a time, stranded for a day or three until what our lookout comrade Skip—aka Eagle Peak—would call "a real toad-strangler" of a storm moved over and swept them down a draw toward the canyon bottom. With a few more days of good precip, a stream would form in the arroyo, tumbling John's remains through pools and carrying them through scalloped riffles as they made their way toward the canyon of the river's Crazy Fork.

There, on autumn nights after fire season had ended and the tourists had all gone home for the summer and the young hippies had packed up their things and returned to school, John liked to set up camp near the stream below a big warm spring. The weather was rarely better in the Gila than in mid-September—warm days, cool nights. In the daytime he would hike or ride Sundance or loaf about the river skipping stones. In the evening, after the sun dropped below the canyon wall, he would arrange tea candles all around the edge of the pool and set them alight so he could sit and soak for hours, miles from the nearest road, while the stars slid across the sky and the flames danced in the steaming surface of the water and the overhanging trees cast undulant shadows that moved like spirits of the ancients as he thought to himself how lucky he was to have found such a spot after a lifetime of footloose wandering. At long last, a proper home in the world. And in the epicenter of untamed fire, the original American Wilderness.

A SONG FOR THE RIVER

MÓNICA AND I WENT to the mountain that summer, a homecoming and a honeymoon. I had been away for nearly two years and prevented from having a full season there for four, what with interventions from the Silver Fire, John's death, and my own corporeal frailty. An absence of 700 days gave my return the feeling of a minor triumph, another small miracle.

It was a quiet fire season, made mellow by unusually heavy rains in early June, when normally the forest was at its driest. On June 7—the four-year anniversary of the Silver Fire and the three-year anniversary of John's death—I looked in on the hueco where I had once spread his ashes and found it full of standing water, inhabited by salamanders. No such thing had ever happened that early in the season, not in my years there. The next day the hueco was dry again, and the salamanders had returned to their burrows. Their brief appearance reminded me that in our restless human quest to make meaning, sometimes all we have to do is pay attention. Meaning will be made for us.

Mónica wished to know the rhythms of the place for herself, to sit at night by an outdoor fire under a sky silly with stars and feel the magisterial hush of dwelling amid the fog in the rainy season.

She quit her job and arrived in mid-June, spent whole afternoons on her belly in the meadow, watching short-horned lizards dine on passing ants and ladybugs converge on sapling pines. We made hot dogs and s'mores to celebrate the solstice American-style. Sticky-fingered and delirious from sugar, we moved off into the dark to watch shooting stars trace their evanescent paths across the long arc of the Milky Way. Alone there on the rim of the range, joined in an odyssey through sky and light, waking to the first bird calls of morning, spooning against the chill of night, we grew closer with every passing day.

Any couple who survives three or four months with no human company but each other is destined for a long permanent relationship. They deserve each other. So wrote the author and fire lookout Edward Abbey, with the caustic irony of a man five times married. I felt quite the opposite. I had done nothing to deserve Mónica, but we had already tested the edges of the phrases *for better or for worse, in sickness and in health.* During my recovery from the hip surgeon's handiwork, I had dabbled with the Percocet he prescribed and sensed almost instantly that down that path lay ruin. Instead, flat on my back in El Paso, I dreamt my way to the mountain: the spooky moonrises over the desert in the east, the bounding deer and blooming irises, the hills flowing through hues of green and blue, gray and black with the circuit of the sun. And when my imagination faltered, Mónica joined me in bed and rubbed my feet, massaged my legs, scratched my head, anything to distract me from my rather pathetic condition.

In a sign of the squalid times, my health insurance plan was discontinued on the day after my second surgery, and the one I bought to replace it denied me coverage for any post-op physical therapy. Mónica proposed marriage in order to bring me under her plan. It made sense. It felt right. We were all in by then anyway, so for the sake of love and my full recovery we held a small ceremony in the backyard, just a few family and friends in attendance, flowers in her hair, pearls at her neck. I could barely stand to utter my vows, but her love was the major reason I came out the other side, and I hoped in time to prove worthy of it.

It would be the work of a lifetime if I could pull it off.

Often in the evenings that summer, we took a long walk off the mountain, alternating between meditation and observation, talking and thinking. Our meanders reminded me that in the forests of the Southwest, no place is more lushly green than a burn scar in recovery: aspen now eight feet tall, riotous tangles of locust with thorns like fish hooks, grama grass and raspberry sprouts and fire-following mosses that sparkled like crushed velvet. Everywhere the country was alive with new growth.

Toward the end of one of our twilight walks, Mónica turned to me and put her finger to her lips. Ahead of us, just off the trail, stood a saffron-colored bear, a male yearling, tipping over rocks in search of worms and grubs. It was Mónica's first such encounter, a moment she had both anticipated and feared. We moved with care, creeping in silence through the grass, keeping a safe distance as we watched him snuffling for food. We admired his beauty and honored his power by letting him drift away down the side of the mountain, unaware of our presence.

A moment together in the presence of a bear: it was a start at balancing the scales. And not the last such encounter of our summer, not the only jolt of joy. There would be other bear sightings, and afternoons of downy fog, and double rainbows over the desert, and surprise visits from friends emerging cold and shivering through the mist—venerable poets grooving on the pain and pleasure of the climb. There were days when four different varieties of hummingbird visited the feeder: rufous, blue-throated, broadtail, calliope. There were opulent hours of reading in the hammock and nights when the tree frogs croaked their mating call, a chorus that seemed to applaud our own amorous instincts.

There were moments when it felt as if we might spontaneously combust from an excess of ecstasy.

I OFTEN HAD OCCASION to wonder that summer how my fellow humans endure the seemingly unendurable. If our culture offers one overriding message, it's that the trick is to avoid looking too hard at anything. Never have a people been so commanded to distraction. Terrorists destroy our gleaming temples of finance and commerce, and our leaders instruct us to go shopping. Our pursuit of new forms of intelligence privileges the artificial. Two billion of us seek validation and connection through a tool that began as a crummy, misogynistic web site called FaceMash whose sole purpose was to rank the hotness of women at Harvard. A visiting sociologist from another planet could easily conclude that the pinnacle of human purpose in our time is expressed in the act of art-directing quirky photo shoots of what we eat for lunch. We exalt "disruption," lionize men who live by the credo "break things." We treat our pain with pills whose end game is to extinguish pain by extinguishing our selves.

As a corrective I sometimes thought of John and Jenny Mahl. When I paid them a visit on my days off the tower that summer, they showed me what remained of Michael's sunglasses collection, most of which they had given away to his friends, little tokens of remembrance. They allowed me to hold his hand-carved didgeridoo, a gorgeous marriage of the creative and the native—his own artistry brought to bear on a sturdy yucca stalk.

Their family once played songs together every evening before dinner, but with Michael gone a silence moved in—a silence, by the time of our meeting, more than three years long. "You know what kind of plane it was that Ritchie Valens, Buddy Holly, and the Big Bopper died in?" John Mahl asked me. "A Beechcraft Bonanza. The day the music died—it felt that way for us too."

Jenny still remembered their last breakfast together, when Michael gave her a hug and said, "Mom, I'm so glad we skipped all that silly teenage stuff." John still remembered how, five days before the crash, Michael had sat with a glass of bourbon and a cigar at his older brother's high-school graduation party, "owning it like a boss. We didn't have to worry about him abusing it. He was already so mature." Immediately after the crash, business dropped off at the family's sign-making shop. It took them a little while to realize that people were afraid of them and their grief. By way of invitation John felt a need to tell a local newspaper reporter, "The Mahls are not toxic." He urged people to come by and see them, give them a hug.

Michael had cultivated a fascination with insects from the time he was a small child. As young as age two, he would sit in the family garden and watch ladybugs for hours on end with a patience that astonished his parents. When his mother first visited the crash site a few months after her son's death, a resident of the nearby trailer park guided her to the place where Michael's body was found. Jenny Mahl found the experience of standing there overwhelming—the thought of her son dying in fear as the plane stalled and went out of control, the son she had spent nearly half of her life protecting from harm. Through the smear of her tears and her shuddering sobs she happened to notice, on the bark of an old juniper tree blackened by the fire started by the crash, a solitary ladybug bigger than any she had ever seen. It was one of many such moments she came to think of as "little Michael winks"—mysterious telegrams of comfort and hope sent from the other side—and it was part of what inspired the Mahl family to gather at his gravesite every year on his birthday, to release a small swarm of mail-order ladybugs in his memory.

Amid the stillness of their home and the fierceness of their grief arrived an invitation to re-examine what they cherished. How to survive inside the silence became the work of their lives. The church to which they belonged, the faith they had inherited, no longer felt adequate to their spiritual needs. Its answers did not jibe with the urgency or complexity of their questions. John's father led that church, so drifting away involved a painful break with family tradition, but such were the demands of an honest reckoning with tragedy. They could not lie to themselves. They could not go through the motions and pretend.

They discovered that their true church, the place where they made contact with the holy, was in the wild Gila. Their son had loved the great fecund pageant of the out of doors, and to be in the presence of insects and wildlife was to feel close to him in a way unattainable inside a box with four walls and a roof. They now made a habit of camping in the woods whenever the demands of their business allowed them the time. Intimacy with the nonhuman not only helped them preserve intimacy with

Michael, it helped them cultivate connection with their two living sons, Alex and Danny, who enjoyed camping too.

Contrary to the dictates of the culture, they had come to understand that the trick was to look harder at everything.

WHEN I LOCKED UP THE CABIN and came down the mountain for the last time that season, I went to the river, where I had people to see and work to witness.

I began on the river's main stem, thirty-five miles northwest of Silver City. I timed my arrival just after six buses of kids unloaded and organized themselves in groups at the Gila River Farm, in the valley below the proposed dam, on a piece of land owned by the Nature Conservancy—eighty acres of river and floodplain. With donations given by friends and admirers of Ella Jaz in the aftermath of the crash, Patrice Mutchnick had set up a watershed conservation fund in her daughter's name. It brought more than 200 Silver City fifth-graders to the river for an afternoon field trip each fall, where they learned about stream ecology. This year, for the first time, the fund provided seed money for matching grants to expand the festival from one day to three, which allowed the organizers to include fifth-graders from other towns near Silver City.

At different stations across the property, instructors taught the kids how to measure turbidity and dissolved oxygen, how to make adobe bricks from river mud, how to weave a duck shape from a cattail reed. Jenny Mahl guided one of the groups of children, and Patrice led the instruction station on pollinators. In an open field the kids played a game that mimicked bird migration. Some imitated cooper's hawks and peregrine falcons. One kid played a hurricane. The rest tried to run the gauntlet as neotropical migrants, eluding predators and harsh weather.

Next to a pond and irrigation canal, Patrice showed the kids how to catch a butterfly in a net for a closeup look at its intricate color pattern. She told the children how she and some other adults had created this place called Butterfly Way, seeded with native flowering plants to attract pollinators vital for our food supply; avocados and apples and other yummy things could not grow without them. Then she sent the kids off with nets and instructions to bring back what they caught to share with the group. They shrieked and laughed as they ran through the field, nets swinging wildly.

Their joy transported me in memory to the high mountains along the border of Michoacán and Mexico state, for by then Mónica and I had fulfilled our vow of seeing the wintering grounds of the monarch butterfly. We had visited with members of an *ejido*—a traditional structure of communal farmland ownership— who were hard at work on strategies for preserving the monarch's habitat: sustainable agriculture, forest protection, responsible ecotourism. I was intrigued to learn that among the ways the *ejido* guarded the oyamel fir forest crucial to the monarchs' survival was to station lookouts in the mountains to sound the alarm against illegal logging. In at least one case, a lookout had been killed by tree poachers. Others had had their lives threatened. I found these stories both sad and inspiring: lookouts who put their lives on the line to protect a landscape they loved, a forest they recognized as precious and irreplaceable, in defiance of men who thought only of short-term profit. Lookouts engaged in the profound work of nurturing inter-species respect.

We rode horseback into the forest to watch the monarchs awaken with the heat of the day. It was the most beautiful thing I had ever seen. We felt as if we had found ourselves inside a snowglobe filled with butterflies—tens of thousands of them swirling like autumn leaves not exactly falling but drifting and floating, and us privileged to sit for a moment inside their riot of color.

To be a native of southern Minnesota, as I am, is to be from a land where men systematically destroyed almost every last wild thing that once enlivened the place. As a child I participated in the transition from the old practice of pulling weeds by hand from the soybean fields to using Roundup herbicide that killed everything it touched. With a spray bottle full of liquid poison, I had walked the rows of beans and laid waste to patches of milkweed that the monarchs depended on for sustenance. Part of my journey to the butterflies' winter home involved an impulse to greet them where they gathered and tell them I was sorry. I expected the moment to be somber, but try being somber inside a snowglobe full of butterflies.

Once the children studied and released their catches, Patrice gathered them around her and calmed them by lowering her voice to just above a whisper. "Let's all turn and look at the pond," Patrice said. The kids complied. "Isn't it pretty? Part of the reason we picked this place to make Butterfly Way was that my daughter loved to come here. She and her friends liked to swim in the pond and teach children like you about the river and the butterflies. We made this place so you could enjoy the beauty just like they did."

She told them, very gently, that her daughter had died in a plane crash with her friends while studying the forest, and that the bench with a memorial plaque on it, next to the pond, helped people remember things that Ella Jaz and her friends had cared about. The children stood rapt, the only time all day they went completely silent.

Patrice urged the group to follow her on a path, single file, to a sycamore tree on the north side of the pond. "This tree is 200 years old," she told them, "older than any of us will ever be. Some things grow very old, and some people die very young, but no matter how long we have, we should try to bring beauty into the world. Give the bark a touch and see how smooth it is. When you feel it, think about things that are important to you. Things you love or think are beautiful."

One by one the children touched the tree. A pale, morose-looking boy, blue-lipped and shivering, waited to be last in line. A few minutes earlier he had broken down in tears, complaining of the cold. Now he placed his palm against the tree and whispered a few words. He fell silent and closed his eyes. When he opened them again, his face softened into a smile.

ON MY WAY UPSTREAM toward the headwaters, I stopped in Silver City for a monthly meeting of the New Mexico Unit of the Central Arizona Project: the CAP Entity, as it was known for short. Created under a joint powers agreement with the Interstate Stream Commission, it was comprised of fourteen voting members, the majority of them representatives of farm irrigation commissions with an interest in the dam. The group would have ultimate responsibility for designing, building, and operating any diversion-dam project on the Gila. But thirteen years after the legislation that made the dam a possibility, and $12 million into work by lawyers, consultants, and engineers fattening at the public trough by committing acts of vandalism against good government, and still there was no defined project, only a vague conviction among all involved that the river had to be dammed, somehow, somewhere.

The project remained a folly in search of a justification, but none of the men around that table had one, other than ancestral spite for Arizona. Their delusions were more entrenched than ever. Their self-interest was so naked as to be embarrassing. They had been convinced by powerful men in Santa Fe that the water was theirs for the taking, a bit of propaganda that gave the push for a dam the character of a moral crusade—never mind that every drop they robbed from the Gila would have an exchange cost attached to it, whereby they would have to pay, at a rate of $160 per acre foot, to deliver Colorado River water to senior rights-holders downstream, in order to replace what was diverted from the Gila. If the diversion dam took 14,000 acre feet per year—the stated goal of its champions—that would add more than $2 million to the project's cost annually.

Members of the CAP Entity almost never mentioned this inconvenient fact. Nor did they acknowledge that, indirectly, a diversion dam at the head of the Gila-Cliff valley would amount to a corporate giveaway: the largest private landowner just downstream was none other than the international mining giant Freeport-McMoRan, which leased most of that land to farmers. Instead they quibbled over where to put the dam, and who would get first crack at the water, and whether it should be stored directly on farms in ponds, or sluiced into a reservoir, or injected underground by some nebulous process of "aquifer recharge." They had finally given up the billion-dollar pipe dream to pump water over the Continental Divide. They had never seriously considered fully funding projects that could have benefited the 60,000 residents of the four-county area targeted for help by the original legislation. Instead they now appeared inclined to build not just one diversion dam, but three—including one on the San Francisco River, a small tributary of the Gila—and all for the sake of bringing subsidized water to a number of farmers who could fit comfortably in a Silver City bar.

For all their high-minded talk, one thing appeared clear. They would eventually do as most men do when handed power and a big pot of free money. They would privilege their own private interests. And to what ultimate purpose? There was no rational answer. An obscure provision in a pork-barrel spending bill had set in motion a process that now moved under its own momentum, making everyone involved a prisoner to another form of mission-completion bias. And the mission, by all appearances, was to spend a big wad of government cash to throw down some concrete in the shape of a middle finger pointed toward Arizona.

EAGER TO BE IN BETTER COMPANY, I fled Silver City and dropped in that evening on the fish biologists, who were in the midst of their annual stream-sampling survey. I found them done with their work for the day, gathered in the kitchen of the bunkhouse at the Heart Bar Wildlife Area, making dinner. The mood of their talk indicated that happy hour was well underway. The minute I walked through the door, the dean of the upper Gila River native-fish biologists, David Propst, handed me a glass. "Fish drink water," he said, "fish biologists drink whisky. I presume you'll join us."

He poured me three fingers of good Scotch, and we sat on the screened porch with his colleagues and their graduate students, paper plates full of salad and barbecued chicken in our laps. Propst, a tall, bespectacled fellow with a salt-and-pepper beard, had been at this work since the 1980s, mostly as a scientist for the New Mexico Department of Game and Fish. He had played a major role in the recovery of the endangered Gila trout, which had nearly gone extinct but now claimed a solid foothold in the headwaters. More recently he had sat on the doctoral committee of James Whitney, a Ph.D student studying food webs in the river—who was eating what and where.

After the big fires hit, the focus of the study shifted. The burns and subsequents floods had offered a chance to examine how native fish respond to historic wildfires in a relatively intact river system. Since Whitney had data on fish populations from before the fires, it made sense to keep collecting and see if they could hazard some answers.

"All of us anticipated really devastating impacts on native fish," Propst said. That fear was initially borne out by the data. After the big burns in 2012 and 2013, their annual survey had found radically diminished numbers of natives—in particular loach minnow and spikedace, both listed under the Endangered Species Act—at all of their sampling sites, and not a single instance of the headwater chub. They began to fear the fish might never recover.

Their survey this year dispelled that fear. It had been, Propst told me, a very good couple of days. On the main stem of the river, downstream of the proposed dam, spikedace and loach minnow appeared in their nets in numbers not seen in years. And in the headwater forks, traditional stronghold of the chub, the sampling effort turned up several of that species in places where it had been completely absent since before the big fires. Propst and one of his research partners, Keith Gido, from Kansas State University, had thirty years of good data on the upper Gila's native and non-native fish, but they admitted they had less of a working theory of what was going on in the watershed than ever. "If you have devastating disturbances, and at all sampling locations you're not finding species, and then all of a sudden they're back, and in some cases superabundant—where are their refugia?" Propst asked. "How do you explain it? I could give you my theory, but I'd be talking like a man with a paper asshole in the middle of a forest fire."

I laughed, and Propst poured us each another glass of Scotch as the conversation continued. The thing the fish had going for them, he said—the major plausible reason for their recovery—could be summed up in one word: connectivity. Somewhere in the watershed, survivors had hung on in little scattered pockets, finding havens amid floodwaters dark with ash and sediment. As the burn scars recovered and the watershed stabilized, the survivors began to leave their refugia and recolonize stretches of the river where the floods had wiped them out.

This connectivity made the upper Gila River unique in the Southwest. So many other streams were dammed up and sucked dry, which fragmented habitat and isolated surviving fish. This in turn eroded genetic diversity in those fish, and with it their resilience to threats such as drought, non-native predators, and floods thick with ash. By comparison, the upper Gila was relatively pristine. Another Ph.D student, Tyler Pilger, had performed a study that found a genetic link between minnow populations in the Gila-Cliff Valley, below the proposed dam, and populations in the headwater tributaries, more than forty miles upstream. To think of minnows making a journey that long boggled my mind. I had found it arduous enough in a boat, moving with the current, and no one along the route had tried to eat me. But DNA tests of fin clips, gathered from netted fish over multiple years during the sampling survey, told the tale. It had happened.

"In a fish population," Propst said, "it's just like with humans. Some have wanderlust. That's what maintains genetic diversity—the wanderers." Building a dam would be like building a wall. If a discreet population in one place suffered punishing effects from drought or ash, they might never recover without connectivity to other populations. And if they died out in a localized extinction, the dam would limit the ability of others to move in and recolonize that reach of stream. The wandering of the wanderers would forever be curtailed.

What is a species more or less among engineers? Aldo Leopold once asked, rhetorically. Among those hell-bent on damming the Gila, I had heard more than one, at a public meeting, proclaim with ignorant certainty that the ash flows in the big floods had totally wiped out minnows whose listed status under the Endangered Species Act might otherwise complicate their wishes. They viewed the fish not, in Leopold's words, as *fellow voyageurs in the odyssey of evolution* and therefore deserving of a place alongside us humans for the long run, but rather as annoying pests whose death at the hands of fire and flood would be no great loss—indeed, would represent a green light to the backhoes.

They were wrong, of course. They had spoken like men with paper assholes in the middle of a forest fire, although they lacked the dignity to admit it. The minnows had proven resilient and, by extension, reaffirmed the resilience of the living river system on which they depended. Maybe, just maybe, we could seek to understand them instead of throwing them on the ash heap of history. Maybe, just maybe, if we left them alone and allowed the river to sustain its wild energies, they would make it through the climate bottleneck of the 21st century, when life is destined to get harder for most living things on Earth. *To keep every cog and wheel is the first precaution of intelligent tinkering*, Leopold also wrote, but one needn't look very hard or very far to see that our species' tinkering generally lacked forethought and caution.

Industrial-size threats to what's left of our natural inheritance are a whack-a-mole phenomenon. David Brower, the founder of the Sierra Club, once said that "the extractive interests—the miners and loggers and dam builders—only have to win once. We have to win every time." So far advocates for a wild upper Gila River had won every time. It still ran as high and fast as snowmelt and rainfall dictated, at least until it met its first immovable obstacle at Coolidge Dam, far down in the desert of Arizona, after which the lower Gila could hardly be called a river at all. Upstream from there the only predictable thing about it was its unpredictability. Maybe that's what irked the schemers and dreamers—that here, in the 21st century, a wild and living thing remained beyond human control.

We had arrived at a moment when any American ideal worth defending was under enormous new threat. That included the hard work of shared ownership in protected public land—indeed the very idea of the commons as a public good, and not merely a profit source awaiting plunder by private interests. Certainly the virtue of humility did not appear ascendant. But humility and the commons were at the heart of what the upper Gila River watershed represented: a place where humanity's industrial tools were kept at bay, to allow the land to be—to simply be—and in the process remain ours to share, not just with future generations but with the marvelous diversity of nonhuman life that preceded us.

If we abandoned that ideal here, in the birthplace of American Wilderness, surely we could abandon it anywhere.

FOR A VISION of interspecies coexistence, I traveled over the Continental Divide into the valley of the Rio Mimbres, a drive of one hour from the Heart Bar. The Mimbres, while small, was a unique stream—a river to nowhere in a land between. Unlike the Gila and the Rio Grande, which carved their separate paths to different oceans, the Mimbres did not pick a side off the Continental Divide. It traveled a slender swath of country down the middle before dying underground in a desert basin east of Deming, fifty miles southeast of Silver City. In the foothills of the Black Range, though, it ran clear and cold, cold enough for trout.

I had been invited there by Ella Myers' sister Raven after seeing her in a Silver City coffee shop, our first encounter in five years. After some initial pleasantries, we had taken up a discussion of our shared membership in an unfortunate club, those of us who've had a sibling die young. We both remembered the way her sister had to be prodded to speak of her writing as we sat together over dinner with mutual friends. Dreams in which the dead reappeared with shocking clarity had been a feature of grief for both of us, and we each knew the feeling of detachment from the world that comes from losing a part of oneself in the loss of a brother or sister.

"I know the one thing she would have wanted was for us to share her artistry with people," Raven said. With that in mind, Raven had pushed her parents to mount a show of Ella's writings, photographs, and short films in Silver City. Later some of Ella's gorgeous, ethereal photos of clouds from that show would appear alongside work from other contemporary artists at Albuquerque's 516 Arts gallery, in a group show called "Landscapes of Life and Death."

Raven showed me some of her own photos from Africa and Mexico, where she had gone on study-abroad trips through WNMU. There she pursued a degree in biology with an emphasis on entomology; her most charismatic images captured extreme close-ups of beetles, her personal passion. Before she ran off to an afternoon class, she invited me to visit her family's farm for a picnic sometime. I immediately accepted.

Along the banks of the Mimbres, on thirty-one acres of riparian bottomlands and juniper-studded hills, her father, Brian, had almost finished building the family's dream home—the most personal expression of his longtime work in construction. He and Raven's mother, Jennifer Douglass, both had careers as visual artists. Jennifer also bred and trained horses and tended a small herd of Navajo-Churro sheep, a heritage breed first brought to North America by the Spanish more than 400 years ago. In an effort to destroy the traditional way of life of the Navajo, the US government had attempted to wipe out the sheep: they were almost lost to extinction by the 1970s. Now Jennifer was helping revive this rare land race of beautiful, desert-adapted creatures. Raven practiced animal husbandry too, raising her own flock of champion show chickens under the name Sky High Sumatras.

The family had lived for years on another small working farm just south of Silver City, but they planned to sell that property and move to the Mimbres with their livestock once Brian finished work on the house.

The shape and character of their Mimbres farm site was the culmination of years of sweat and planning. They had owned the property since 2008, but first it had to be cleared of the detritus left by the previous owner—a hoarder of some renown. "Nothing ever left here," Brian said. "Things came in and all of them stayed. We had to haul them away by the ton." Most of it was irredeemable junk, but amid the cleanup they found a few treasures that remained useful. The previous house on the property had burned in a structure fire. Brian salvaged some of the lumber from the porch for use in a barn he also built with his own two hands. He pointed to certain planks marked by char along their edges. Making use of them had been a way to recycle available materials, but it was more than that. Those blackened boards gestured to the history of the place. They braided threads of heritage from past to present.

"Beauty from the burn," I said.

"It gives the thing some character, doesn't it?" he said.

Horses had been a constant presence in their lives for two decades. Jennifer described how Ella had spent every day with her and the animals, in the barns and the pasture, from the time she was a baby. "Even as a little girl she had an eye for horses," Jennifer said. "She could ride anything. As soon as she would get on a horse's back, the horse would settle. She had a calmness about her that animals responded to."

Years earlier they had gone to Tucson to have a look at a Dutch mare they were warned was a spirited creature. They watched from the edge of a ring while the horse leapt and snorted and tossed her head like a diva, prancing and dancing and showing off. She was seventeen hands tall, beautiful, and totally unrideable. They knew immediately they had to have her. They took her home, named her Gracie, and after a year of training she became Ella's horse. The girl and the horse fell in love. They rode together almost every day, galloping across the landscape around their farm.

The care and training of horses gave the family a shared experience rooted in the physicality of animate flesh, and as artists Jennifer and Brian encouraged conversation on matters of creativity and intellectual ambition. But it came as a revelation for them to confront Ella's hidden inner life in the journals she left behind. Many times she wrote of an urgency she felt to create, and an apprehension of time slipping away. *As a child I spent most of my free time riding horses*, she wrote, less than a month before her death. *The summers were endless. Now summers are so short. It's strange [that] time seemed so slow when I was young, but now, now things seem to be going too fast for me to ever catch up. Every year goes by faster. Every year brings me closer to an end I know deep inside me is there but which I cannot see. I feel like every day my time is running out and I'm powerless to do anything… I'm realizing that those things that are temporary are the most beautiful… I don't know, life is a strangely beautiful devastating thing.*

On the day Ella died, as a favor of the sort friends do in such moments, a woman named Tammy looked in on the family's horses to make sure they were fed and watered. She found Gracie out of her mind in a full white lather, whinnying so loud it sounded like screaming. "Tammy tried to calm her down but nothing worked,"

Jennifer said. "Gracie was rearing and running in circles, just a total basketcase. Somehow she knew Ella was gone."

After Ella's death, Jennifer adopted Gracie as her own, and the horse barn became both her sanctuary and her hell, a place so thick with meaning and memory, so dense with presence and absence, she could barely stand it. Gracie offered her a tangible connection to Ella. Sometimes they would be out on the landscape, riding like any other day, and all of a sudden something would shift, and a calmness would flow through them like water. "It was as if time would stop, or if not stop at least cease to matter, you know what I mean? We were in some other place without time. I knew Gracie could feel it too. She would float almost like she wasn't even touching the ground—and in that moment I knew Ella was with us."

Two weeks before my visit, Gracie had fallen ill with a bad case of colic, and Jennifer had taken her to the veterinarian. The vet treated her for a blockage in her intestine and told Jennifer to keep a close eye on her. Gracie had always had colic problems, but this time was worse. She couldn't seem to recover, and her nights became terrible as she thrashed about in pain. Jennifer took her to the vet a second time and had her suspicion confirmed. Gracie was not going to get better, not this time. Jennifer had long ago made a promise to Ella that she would never allow Gracie to suffer, and although it meant losing her major private connection to her daughter, she gave the vet the go-ahead to put Gracie down.

"Normally I would have been there for it," Jennifer said. "I just couldn't do it this time. I could feel the moment of her death, though. A sense of peace came over me. A sense of calm and gratitude. Gracie by her nature demanded attention from me every day for three years. She's probably the reason I survived."

Years of experience with animals—Jennifer and her horses and sheep, Raven and her chickens—had taught the family just how deep cross-species communication could go. Unlike some farmers, they never treated their livestock with a heavy hand. The animals were allowed personalities, allowed to show love and fear. "And man, do they show love if you let them," Jennifer said. "Our stallions were crazy about Gracie, and how could you blame them? She was so flamboyant. They would prance and squeal for her, and when our lambs got out, they would go eat in the stall with her. She was so gentle with them, almost like a mother. We have two lambs named Frick and Frack, and they liked to sleep with Gracie. It was so sweet to watch them together."

To farm well requires an elaborate courtesy toward all creatures, Wendell Berry wrote, and along the banks of the Mimbres the family planned to continue an experiment in the cultivation of courtesy. Several rare or endangered species occupied the property, from Chihuahuan chubs and Chiricauhua leopard frogs to willow flycatchers, yellow-billed cuckoos, and common black hawks. Many private property owners would stay mum about such creatures—or drive them off, fearful of government interference in their livelihood. Not here.

"We view it as a blessing and an opportunity," Jennifer said. "We want to keep migratory routes open, so animals can move through the property, and we plan buffer zones around the livestock impacts." They would fence off the river bottom to keep the sheep and horses from damaging the riparian area. They would aim to live and work in such a way as to preserve and even encourage the biotic richness and diversity of their land. They would not measure its value in dollars alone but in how many of their fellow creatures thrived alongside them. They imagined the place evolving over time into a multi-use education center with workshops on green building methods, conservation biology, nature writing—ways of sharing what they learned with others, building community, celebrating connectivity among humans and creatures alike.

"We've suffered the hardest lesson you can learn in impermanence and ephemerality," Jennifer said. "It truly shattered us." But they had managed to put the pieces back together—and they were going to do their utmost to nurture the life that was here before them and would remain, if they had any say in the matter, long after they were gone.

I MARKED THE TRANSITION of seasons with a week at the Swede's old haunt, once again reacquainting myself with its healing waters: the hot spring seeps and soaking tubs, the cool, clear stream. Cottonwoods along the banks were turning yellow, one last flaring before shedding their leaves; summer was giving way to autumn and the light had turned, the midday shadows longer and softer at the edges.

After ten years in the Gila region, the Swede had decided it was time to move on to a new phase of life, so I had the place to myself with the blessing of Frank's youngest son, Aari, maker of the perfect martini. Last I saw the Swede he told me he had booked a flight to Hawaii to spend time with his daughter and her family on the beach at Kailua, play chess with his grandchildren, help build a little guesthouse on their property. "I'm going to buy myself a snow-white suit made of hemp and a good pair of sandals," he said, "and sit on the beach nursing a cocktail with a little pink umbrella in it, and I'm going to caress my illusions and cultivate my eccentricities. I'm too old to be fixing leaky water lines with Mormon rawhide and baling wire. But I trust you'll look in there from time to time. And I hope you'll say hi to Frank on the mesa for me." He said this very intently, with a tone of supplication normally foreign to his being.

On my last night there, I did as he asked. Seated next to Frank's grave, the river below me glowing like a phosphorescent snake in the moonlight, I drank a glass of bourbon, smoked a cigar, and thought of Michael Mahl and his father's description of him at his brother's graduation party, glass of whisky in one hand, cigar in the other, "owning it like a boss." What a way to be remembered. What pain and pride I had heard in the voice that said those words.

I poured a little out on Frank's grave and told him the Swede sent his regards. Through the Swede's stories I had come to know Frank a little. I discovered more when, with the blessing of Frank's sons, I looked through a box of his papers left behind at the ranch after his death. Its contents offered a hint of why a man with a glamorous life in San Francisco in the Age of Aquarius might choose one day, at the height of his success, to give it all up and retreat to the wilds of New Mexico.

In a document titled "Life History," Frank wrote:

I was born in Cologne, Germany, in 1929. When Hitler came to power in 1933, my father and mother and I were living in Essen, Germany. My father had been an international trade executive, traveling across Europe on trading and banking missions. My father took my mother and me and walked across the frontier to Holland to escape Nazi retribution since he had been actively involved in anti-

Hitler activities and was a prime target. The only possession he took along was his camera which became his new source of employment. By 1935 we had settled in Antwerp, Belgium, where my mother died. This was a great shock to my father, and I have been told by their friends that if it had not been for his son, he might have killed himself.

Father and son were forced to flee again when the Nazis overran the lowlands on May 10, 1940. Of this chaotic time Frank remembered *crowded refugee trains, bombing by the Luftwaffe, and finally being overrun by the German armies somewhere in France. After being shuttled from camp to camp in cattle cars, we wound up in St. Cyprien, a concentration camp previously built to house Spanish loyalists. Through extremely fortunate circumstances, we were able to escape just prior to being shipped to the extermination camps of Germany. With the help of friends and my father's sister in New York, we eventually arrived in New York City, via Marseilles, Africa, and Martinique.*

I once asked the Swede what "extremely fortunate circumstances" may have allowed for that escape from St. Cyprien, and he told me he had no idea. In their decades of friendship, Frank had uttered not a word about his childhood.

In America, Frank and his father lived an itinerant existence until Frank joined the Navy in 1948. He received an honorable discharge the following year, and *after this there came about a year of drifting. This was pre-Jack Kerouac but it was "on the road" through Texas.* In Dallas, police picked him and a buddy up on a vagrancy charge, held them in jail three days, and ran them out of town with instructions never to return.

Frank made his way to San Francisco by late 1950. After an early career as a photographer like his father, he became the publicist for the Purple Onion and Hungry i nightclubs. He produced a long-running play with Charles Schulz based on Schulz's "Peanuts" comic, opened a restaurant and record-production company, launched the Kingston Trio to superstardom, and mingled with Woody Allen, Allen Ginsberg, and Alan Watts. His first wife ran off with Lenny Bruce, a frequent performer at the Purple Onion. He gave a then-unknown aspiring comic named Robin Williams a job as a busboy in his famous Sausolito hot spot, the Trident. When Frank was busted with those six sea bags full of weed at his plush pad on De Silva Island in 1968, the *San Francisco Chronicle* went with a double-decker, banner headline on its front page: *Fantastic Dope Case: The Swinging Tycoon—Showman Seized in Huge Pot Raid.* Among those who testified at trial on his behalf were a pastor, a rabbi, and the comedian Tommy Smothers, who admitted that smoking grass with Frank helped him "untwist the knots."

"I've seen the world and had my share of good times," the Swede once told me, "but sitting in Alan Watts's houseboat on Richardson Bay, smoking a doobie with him and Frank while they talked philosophy—it never got better than that."

Watts, who wrote numerous popular books on Eastern philosophy, as well as the ever topical *The Wisdom of Insecurity: A Message for an Age of Anxiety*, died when he was just fifty-nine years old, in 1973, after a grueling lecture tour. The death of his good friend shook Frank to his core. Around that time he began to question what he wanted from the rest of his days on Earth. I wondered whether it wasn't just his friend's death but his friend's words that inspired a reexamination of values. In *The Wisdom of Insecurity*, Watts wrote: *Our age is one of frustration, agitation, and addiction to dope. Somehow we must grab what we can, while we can, and drown out the realization that the whole thing is futile and meaningless. This "dope" we call our high standard of living, a violent and complex stimulation of the senses, which makes them progressively less sensitive and thus in need of yet more violent stimulation. We crave distraction—a panorama of sights, sounds, thrills and titillations into which as much as possible must be crowded in the shortest possible time.*

Whatever the prod, Frank began his search for a retreat from the world he had made for himself, a world of real-estate investments, record deals, and nonstop parties. What he wanted, it turned out, was the one thing he had been denied in his formative years as a young Jewish boy on the run for his life across Europe: a home he could call his own. The one he found was completely defensible, with the same road in as out, and a number of neighbors within three miles he could count on the fingers of one hand. A place where the ancient secrets still murmured in the meeting of stone and water.

I failed to see how he could have done better and I told him so, there on the mesa amid the moonglow on the river flow, a half-drunk man babbling to the dead—a habit some judged disreputable.

To me it felt more natural all the time.

IN THE MORNING I drained the tubs and tidied the bunkhouse and drove off for one more visit to a friend.

Patrice Mutchnick met me at the door of her home in Gila Hot Springs and invited me in. I had brought us each a cup of ice cream from Doc Campbell's Post just up the road, and we sat on the porch and visited awhile, catching up on our summer doings.

It had taken me a long time to approach her after the crash, too long by any reasonable standard of condolence—two years, it turned out, although one year of that could be blamed on my odyssey through temporary physical ruin. I had mostly wanted to tell her that her daughter inspired me. What had been so difficult about that? I suppose I feared articulating my feeling of responsibility to Ella Jaz's work in defense of the river because I knew I lacked her poise and clarity on the issue. By uttering aloud my admiration of her activism to the woman who loved her most, I would be bound to honor a promise I had made in the privacy of my own mind, a promise to amplify Ella Jaz's voice in whatever small way I could. I suppose I feared, as well, being burned by drawing too near the heat of a mother's grief. I had watched my own mother grieve for a lost son, saw how elusive words of solace could be. That didn't mean the words would come easier for me. I knew too well the futility of words in the face of such loss.

Despite my fears, Patrice had welcomed me when I first went to see her. She immediately suggested we go to the river, to swim in a place where she had often gone with Ella Jaz. *When it hurts we return to the banks of certain rivers,* the poet Czeslaw Milosz wrote, but the inverse was true too: sometimes returning to the banks of certain rivers makes it hurt. It hurt to swim as two when we ought to have been swimming as three. It hurt for me to tell her that her daughter had inspired me, and it hurt far worse for her to hear it, because I couldn't use the present tense in telling her so. But something about swimming in the river, reveling in the reek of it, that plump, green-brown stink of all that grows and rots near moving water, also made the hurt hurt less.

It was always there, but she had struggled against it by honoring her daughter's passions in every way she could. She brought together various musician friends to record an album of Ella Jaz's songs. She partnered with a filmmaker to shoot a documentary that celebrated Ella, Michael, and Ella Jaz's lives even as it looked unflinchingly at their deaths. She led a project to remove non-native tamarisk from a forty-mile stretch of the river from Gila Hot Springs through the Wilderness and out the other side. She hunted for rare plants in the forest, tagged monarch butterflies for the sake of learning more about their migration pattern.

There in the river we began a conversation we resumed off and on for more than a year. We spoke of death and memory, the lines tragedy carves on a life, the imperative to find beauty amid ruin, how certain songs with deep associations both wound and soothe, how sunny days can feel an insult, human laughter a taunt. She always received me graciously, and I tried to make sure she knew I wasn't some bloodless documentarian conducting a close study of other people's suffering. The truth was, I liked her. I came to admire her, just as I had admired her daughter, though for different reasons. Certain people insinuated that I ought to keep my distance because she had gone a little crazy in her grief. I would have been alarmed if she hadn't—not only for the fact of losing an only daughter and best friend, but for suffering such a loss in the fish bowl of a small town, with no place to hide and everyone staring at you with garish and distorted faces. To judge her disapprovingly seemed to my mind a kind of feint, an excuse for not taking seriously her demand for a full accounting of the events that led to her daughter's death—as if she were supposed to crawl in a hole and stay there mute until she too went to the other side.

That was not her style. She had a tenacity about her that

people praise in men but find threatening in women. She had applied that tenacity to the push for a full investigation of the facts of the crash, an investigation that some in the community judged a vengeful attempt to extract a pound of flesh because it involved, in the end, a legal reckoning. She didn't care. It wasn't about her. It was about the memory of her daughter and the education of the children who would pass through the doors of that school in the years to come.

"Ella loved the school," Patrice said. "She believed in its mission. It encouraged her passions. I know she would have demanded that people own up to the mistakes they made and try to do better in the future, for the sake of the kids. And not out of spite—out of love. That's who she was."

She was also a writer with an uncanny gift of expression for someone her age. On a web site where Patrice posted some of Ella Jaz's personal journals, I found this, under the title "Cord Fluidity":

Most often, I find truths about myself not with someone else, but in the moments alone; seeing a curve of water, knowing no one else will ever see that same drop of water in the same spot again.

Truth is hard to capture, to hold; like a firefly buzzing around the dark chamber of my cupped hands.

Sometimes I see it in a smile, a certain feeling of elation; the plunge of cord fluidity when I'm submerged.

Sometimes as a memory, one I hold close or laugh about with someone else.

A quick spark between the two of us, both remembering the same thing.

At night in my room, my breath the only thing keeping me company, my thoughts go on and on with nothing to bounce off, nothing to curb them.

In a way, that's how I would like to live—free of things to stop my thoughts.

But then I know my thoughts would soon lose their dimension with no interactions to shape them, no other voice to challenge them, or fortify them.

I loved the doubleness of her line of thought, the proposition first stated, then complicated, then amended. You could see her mind at work, writing about the way her mind worked: her words had an unselfconscious beauty about them, like a musician glimpsed unawares, practicing alone, totally absorbed in the act of creation. And that lovely, mysterious phrase, *cord fluidity*: what did it mean? Its ambiguity, its strangeness, lit the imagination. I thought of a diver piercing the surface of a pool, her limbs relaxing afterward. I thought of seaweed undulating with the tide.

I thought of ash carried in a current.

The essence of Ella Jaz's message for the world came down to the fundamental connectedness of every living thing on Earth. Perhaps all the evidence I needed of that truth was that her voice still lived inside of me like a tiny, unwavering flame—a flame I had seen reflected in a butterfly's wing in Michoacán. So often my mind came back to the brutal injustice of all she had left unwritten, all we were denied when her life was cut short—not to mention all the songs Michael Mahl might have sung, all the novels Ella Myers might have written. But to think of them having been denied longer lives in terms of the rest us being denied the fruits of their artistry was to make the tragedy ours and not theirs. That may simply be a fundamental fact embedded in the experience of tragedy: that the living are left to feel the weight of what the dead have left undone.

When we finished our ice cream, Patrice asked, "Do you still want to go visit Ella?"

"Yes," I said, "I was hoping to. I have some things I want to tell her."

She beckoned me to follow. We walked through the back gate of her property and into the late-day shadow cast by the ridge above us. For 200 yards we followed a trail that ran parallel to the ridge, with the river down the valley to our left, the ridge above us on the right. At a certain point we left the trail and began a scramble up the rocky slope, sometimes dropping to all fours to keep our footing. Loose stones skittered down the hill behind us.

The top of the ridge was narrow but flat, its even contour occasionally interrupted by rock formations like terraced wedding cakes. Below us the green gallery forest along the river revealed its path through the valley. Scattered rooftops glinted in the little village along its banks. To the west the high ridges of the Diablos rose jagged and timbered at the head of Little Creek. To the north and east we could see the canyons of the river's headwaters.

We arrived at a small piñon pine. Patrice crouched and placed her hand on a flat, maroon-colored rock. I watched her fingers trace the words carved into it:

Ella Jaz
Fly Free

After a moment she stood and looked at me. She shrugged her day pack from her shoulder. She unzipped it, reached inside, and withdrew a small wooden bowl with a lid held on by clear tape. She handed me the bowl and said, "I trust you'll know what to do with this. I'll leave you alone with Ella and hike back down the long way."

I watched her leave along the ridge trail headed north. When she disappeared from view, I sat down next to the piñon.

I surveyed the offerings scattered about the base of the tree: a tiny stuffed koala, a carved wooden bear the size of my palm. Seashells and crystals and brilliantly colored stones. A mule deer's antler point. A raven's feather. A hummingbird made of beads.

Like Patrice, I traced my fingers along the letters in the maroon rock. I removed the tape from the lid on the bowl and looked inside.

Some ashes of Ella Jaz.

I knew too well what to do. I dipped my fingers in the bowl. I sprinkled a pinch of ash on the rock. I licked my fingertip and savored the bitter taste. I began to weep at the enormity of the honor Patrice had done me, the almost unbearable intimacy of holding her daughter's remnants in my hands. I sobbed until my vision clouded over with tears that fell on the rock and dimpled the dusting of ash, the first tiny movement of their journey joined with rain toward the river.

The Puebloan peoples of northern New Mexico, with a nearly 2,000-year history rooted in the land, view a watershed as a cycle of life—one that encompasses the sky where the water originates, the shape of the Earth where the water percolates and flows, the rocks that erode to create soil, the plants that grow from that soil, and the creatures who subsist on the seeds and fruits of those plants. Eventually the water evaporates into sky, and the cycle begins again.

The ebb and flow of drought and flood are like the pulse in a human body, water moving like blood, carrying nutrients through the veins and arteries of creeks and rivers. We are mostly water too, which explains why not much remains when we burn: a few handfuls of ash. Perhaps that's why it feels natural for ash to join with water. It is a form of reconstitution.

I remembered Patrice questioning me when I used the word remnants about the portion of Ella Jaz's ashes that had joined with the river three years earlier. "Are they remnants or are they seeds?" she wondered.

Maybe both, I came to think: a vestige of a life transfigured by heat into sustenance for some other. A fish. A tree.

Once more I spoke aloud across the divide:

We miss you, Ella Jaz, but we are still here speaking up for the river. We remember your words in defense of it. I hope you won't mind if I borrow some for a story I'm trying to tell. They can't be repeated enough. They teach us still. I even have a few of them down by heart. *We can never separate ourselves from the fate of any other creature or the fate of our planet. We are all in this together for better or worse.* Your exuberant creed stays with me too. *So many people live with their minds closed off to the world. Sealed and safe and complacent. You know what? I want to live a kick-ass life!... I want to scream and cry and laugh and run and dance and eat ice cream and climb mountains and I want to love.*

The world is catching up with you, Ella Jaz. We are learning more all the time about how to love. Would you believe we've begun granting rights to rivers as the equal of humans? Just this year the Māori in New Zealand won legal recognition of the

Whanganui River as an ancestor of their people, and the Ganges has been granted personhood under the laws of India. We're starting to see our fates as intertwined with the lives of rivers. Our laws are playing catch-up with our spirits and our hearts.

One day, hopefully soon, we'll all gather and celebrate one more memorial for one more death. This time it will be a wished-for death, a welcome death, one that's really a reprieve into life: the death of the dream of a dam on the Gila. I can see us already. We'll meet on the banks of the river with all our friends and join hands and sing a song you sang yourself and recorded for posterity. I turn to it when my spirits are low, cuing you up on my CD player, that old gospel standard that invites sisters and brothers, fathers and mothers and sinners too—heaven knows we need it—down to the river:

I went down to the river to pray,
Studying about that good old way,
And who shall wear the starry crown,
Good Lord, show us the way.

Oh sisters, let's go down,
Let's go down, come on down.
Oh sisters, let's go down,
Down to the river to pray…

All of us will be there in the water, joined once more in tears and laughter, gathered in memory of you and your friends, in celebration of all you loved and others we've loved and lost. We'll scream and cry and laugh and swim and dance and eat ice cream and together we'll sing us a song—a song of triumph, a song of love.

A song for the river.

CATECHISM FOR A FIRE LOOKOUT

We will be nearly finished, I think, when we stop understanding the old pull toward green things and living things, toward dirt and rain and heat and what they spawn.

    —John Graves

It doesn't take much in the way of body and mind to be a lookout. It's mostly soul.

    —Norman Maclean

I am glad I shall never be young without wild country to be young in. Of what avail are forty freedoms without a blank spot on the map?

    —Aldo Leopold

I talk to myself and look at the dark trees, blessedly neutral. So much easier than facing people, than having to look happy, invulnerable, clever.

    —Sylvia Plath

As for lightning and fires, who, what American individual loses, when a forest burns, and what did Nature do about it for a million years up to now?

    —Jack Kerouac

If you live, live free / or die like the trees, standing up.
—Mahmoud Darwish

Often the mountain gives itself most completely when I have no destination, when I reach nowhere in particular, but have gone out merely to be with the mountain as one visits a friend.
—Nan Shepherd

A life confined to what is personal is likely, sooner or later, to become unbearably painful; it is only by windows into a larger and less fretful cosmos that the more tragic parts of life become endurable.
—Bertrand Russell

For thousands of years after our race opted for a civilized existence, we dreamed of and labored toward an escape from the anxieties of a wilderness condition only to find, when we reached the promised land of supermarkets and air conditioners, that we had forfeited something of great value.
—Roderick Nash

Isn't it curious that science never invents antidotes? There is no means of spreading silence, or of spreading darkness.
—Sylvia Townsend Warner

Thank God, they cannot cut down the clouds!
—Henry David Thoreau

It's okay to love something bigger than yourself without fearing it. Anything worth loving is bigger than we are anyway.
　　　　　—Percival Everett

After so much constraint and clever politics, alone, removed from men's eyes and instinctively having no fear… he gave himself up to the pleasure of living, so intense at his age, and in the midst of the most beautiful mountains in the world.
　　　　　—Stendhal

In order to understand the world, one has to turn away from it on occasion.
　　　　　—Albert Camus

I try to respect the difficult job of agencies… who think they have to manage every inch of wild country in order to protect it. Maybe they do. I try to keep a balanced view, valuing freedom most. Not freedom to molest and trample but freedom to take total control for your own ass. Even if a bear chews it off: no lawsuits, please.
　　　　　—Doug Peacock

I wondered why it was that places are so much lovelier when one is alone.
　　　　　—Daphne du Maurier

It is perhaps impossible for a person living unhappily with a flush toilet to imagine a person living happily without one.
　　　　　—Wendell Berry

The idea of wilderness… is the most radical in human thought—more radical than Paine, than Marx, than Mao. Wilderness says: Human beings are not paramount, Earth is not for Homo sapiens alone, human life is but one life form on the planet and has no right to take exclusive possession.

—Dave Foreman

In small doses melancholy, alienation, and introspection are among life's most refined pleasures.

—Rebecca Solnit

Why should we tolerate a diet of weak poisons, a home of insipid surroundings, a circle of acquaintances who are not quite our enemies, the noise of motors with just enough relief to prevent insanity? Who would want to live in a world which is just not quite fatal?

—Rachel Carson

Natural objects—living things in particular—are like a language we only faintly remember. It is as if creation had been dismembered sometime in the past and all things are limbs we have lost that will make us whole only if we can recall them.

—Lewis Hyde

If we are here for any good purpose at all (other than collating texts, running rivers, and learning the stars), I suspect it is to entertain the rest of nature. A gang of sexy primate clowns. All the little critters creep in close to listen when human beings are in a good mood and willing to play some tunes.

—Gary Snyder

I am here alone for the first time in weeks, to take up my "real" life again at last. That is what is strange—that friends, even passionate love, are not my real life unless there is time alone in which to explore and to discover what is happening or has happened.

—May Sarton

By speaking of greater forces than we can possibly invoke, and by confronting us with greater spans of time than we can possibly envisage, mountains refute our excessive trust in the man-made. They pose profound questions about our durability and the importance of our schemes. They induce, I suppose, a modesty in us.

—Robert MacFarlane

To have passed through life and never experienced solitude is to have never known oneself. To have never known oneself is to have never known anyone.

—Joseph Wood Krutch

We need the possibility of escape as surely as we need hope; without it the life of the cities would drive all men into crime or drugs or psychoanalysis.

—Edward Abbey

Adieu to disappointment and spleen. What are men to rocks and mountains?

—Jane Austen

To be left alone is the most precious thing one can ask of the modern world.

—Anthony Burgess

The mountains were his masters. They rimmed in life. They were the cup of reality, beyond growth, beyond struggle and death. They were his absolute unity in the midst of eternal change.
—Thomas Wolfe

The idea of the contented hermit who lives close to nature, cultivates his garden and his bees, is trusted by animals and loves all of creation, is some kind of archetype. We think we could be like that ourselves if somehow things were different.
—Isabel Colgate

Crane your neck. Worm your way. Wolf it down. Monkey with things. Outfox your foe. Quit badgering your tax attorney. Take notes on the deafness of coral, the pea-size heart of a bat. Be meticulous. We will need these things so that we may speak.
—Ellen Meloy

Solitude… is the one deep necessity of the human spirit to which adequate recognition is never given in our codes. It is looked upon as a discipline or penance, but hardly ever as the indispensable, pleasant ingredient it is to ordinary life, and from this want of recognition come half our domestic troubles.
—Freya Stark

We are no longer frightened of nature; what frightens us is the idea that we have triumphed over nature, and what that triumph will mean in the long run, when we understand, too late, that we were nature, that our triumph has been a suicide.
—John Jeremiah Sullivan

There is greater comfort in the substance of silence than in the answer to a question.

—Thomas Merton

Elsewhere the sky is the roof of the world; but here the earth was the floor of the sky. The landscape one longed for when one was far away, the thing all about one, the world one actually lived in, was the sky, the sky!

—Willa Cather

It takes a lot of time to be a genius, you have to sit around so much doing nothing, really doing nothing.

—Gertrude Stein

I grow into these mountains like a moss. I am bewitched.

—Peter Matthiessen

You cannot protect your solitude if you cannot make yourself odious.

—E.M. Cioran

Some people see scars, and it is wounding they remember. To me they are proof of the fact that there is healing.

—Linda Hogan

Before there was any water there were tides of fire.

—Robinson Jeffers

If you're lonely when you're alone, you're in bad company.

—Jean-Paul Sartre

Once in his life a man ought to concentrate his mind upon the remembered earth, I believe. He ought to give himself up to a particular landscape in his experience, to look at it from as many angles as he can, to wonder about it, to dwell upon it. He ought to imagine that he touches it with his hands at every season and listens to the sounds that are made upon it. He ought to imagine the creatures that are there and all the faintest motions in the wind. He ought to recollect the glare of noon and all the colors of dawn and dusk.

—N. Scott Momaday

Teach us to care and not to care / Teach us to sit still

—T.S. Eliot

The body is not important. It is made of dust; it is made of ashes. It is food for the worms. The winds and the waters dissolve it and scatter it to the four corners of the earth. In the end, what we care most for lasts only a brief lifetime, and then there is eternity. Time forever… The body becomes dust and trees and exploding fire, it becomes gaseous and disappears, and still there is eternity. Silent, unopposed, brooding, forever.

—Rudolfo Anaya

ACKNOWLEDGMENTS

I am indebted to the families of Ella Myers, Michael Mahl, and Ella Jaz Kirk for permission to quote from each of their writings. For more writing and music by Ella Jaz, visit her web site at www.ellajazkirk.org.

The seeds of this story first sprouted in columns for the *Silver City Daily Press*, where publisher Nick Seibel allowed me to say whatever was on my mind twice a month for most of a year.

An essay-length elegy under the title "Burn Scars," later reworked to form major portions of the book, appeared in the Spring 2016 issue of *n+1*. I am more thankful than I can say for the magazine's support of my writing over the past decade. In this case, I especially wish to acknowledge the editorial assistance of Chad Harbach, Dayna Tortorici, and Nikil Saval.

Other small portions of the book appeared in *Orion,* the *New York Times Magazine*, and the *Los Angeles Times*, where in each case I had the pleasure of working with a shrewd editor. I wish to express my gratitude to Andrew Blechman, Charlie Homans, and Susan Brenneman, respectively.

More people than I can name contributed to my education about the Gila River and the diversion dam that would harm it. But I am particularly indebted for stories shared by, and adventures shared with, the Bruemmer family, Keith (the Guru) Knadler, Alex Tager, Nathan Newcomer, Mark Allison, Bo Hunter, Allyson Siwik, Martha Cooper, Donna Stephens, Todd Schulke,

Norm Gaume, Dutch Salmon, David Propst, Keith Gido, Tyler Pilger, James Whitney, and Jim Brooks. John Fayhee graciously shared documents pertaining to the Signal Fire investigation. Any omissions or errors are my doing, not theirs.

Numerous friends, and friends of friends, opened their homes and shared stories of those memorialized herein. The book profited immeasurably from the contributions of Teresa Beall, Jean Stelzer, Rázik Majean, Sara Irving, Mark Hedge, Patrice Mutchnick, Jenny Mahl, John Mahl, Jennifer Douglass, Brian Myers, Raven Myers, Steve Blake, Maddy Alfero, Mark Johnson, Keith Matthes, and Hans Johansson.

To the lovely people at Cinco Puntos Press who made the creation of this book a singular pleasure and an education in the art of collaboration—Lee Byrd, Bobby Byrd, John Byrd, Anne Giangiulio, Mary Fountaine, Jessica Powers, and Jill Bell—I offer a wish for *salud, dinero, y amor*. They earned that and much more.

The Right Reverend Rigatoni at the Rancho Relaxo offered tequila, life coaching, cowboy poetry, and shelter from the storm at moments when I needed them. *Gracias, cabron.*

Lee Gruber, Chris and Larry McDaniel, Bill and Cindy Neely, the Werber family, Benjamin Alire Sáenz, Alfredo Corchado, Angela Kocherga, the PEN Writers' Fund, the Authors League Fund, the Haven Foundation, and the n+1 Foundation all provided support of one sort or another at crucial junctures. Without them this book would not be.

Most of all, I thank my *corazón*, Mónica Ortiz Uribe— without whom I would not be.

The bear flashed his rump
as he crashed off through the brush—
No need for new friends.

I called in a smoke,
but it was the missile range—
Rehearsing end times.

Dead snags all around,
relics of the old forest—
Woodpeckers love them.

Even on lookout,
amorous forenoons go wrong—
Spoiled by day hikers.

Lost in the mountains,
move as if you were water—
You shall soon be found.

PHILIP CONNORS was born in Iowa, raised on a farm in Minnesota, educated at the University of Montana, and disillusioned by a stint of corporate journalism in New York. He is the author of two previous books: *Fire Season* and *All the Wrong Places*. His work has won the National Outdoor Book Award, the Reading the West Award for nonfiction, the Sigurd Olson Nature Writing Award, and the Grand Prize at the Banff Mountain Book Competition. He lives and works in the U.S. / Mexico borderlands.